"This handbook is a must-have tool for all churches and congregations. It gives step-by-step instructions on how to prepare for a disaster, what to do when a disaster hits and how the church and its congregation can establish care, comfort and support to those recovering from disasters. Ephesians 2:10 states, 'For we are God's workmanship, created in Christ Jesus to do good works that he has prepared in advance for us to do.' I believe this handbook will be a blessing for you and your church in times of disasters."
Ron Willett, director, World Renew Disaster Response Services

"When local churches are hit with an unexpected disaster in their community they often find themselves in uncharted territory, overwhelmed by needs, expectations and demands from both those who need help and those who are offering it. This was our experience in Japan after the 2011 tsunami brought devastation to a large portion of the country. HDI came alongside the churches in Japan to not only meet immediate needs for training but also to learn from the experience to prepare for disasters in the future. This book is the result of listening to those who have gone through the fire, both in Japan and in other disasters such as Haiti, Hurricane Katrina and Typhoon Haiyan in the Philippines, and I believe that this practical research will allow the church to respond with greater effectiveness when disaster strikes again."
Jonathan Wilson, executive director, Christian Relief, Assistance, Support and Hope (CRASH Japan), author of *How Christian Volunteers Can Respond to Disaster*

"A large part of the world's population lives in disaster-prone areas, but communities are often ill prepared when disasters hit. The local church—often situated in the center of communities—can become a great resource in disaster response or even in prevention. We have seen encouraging examples of that, such as when the earthquake destroyed Christchurch or the typhoon hit the Philippines. This book will help churches understand their potential contribution. I recommend it to the leadership of every evangelical alliance as a road map for developing a disaster response in their nation. What an impact it will have to hurting communities, when in the face of widespread despair the body of Christ is ready to serve and combines high competence in practical help with the love of Christ."
Dr. Wilf Glasser, associate secretary general, World Evangelical Alliance

"This is a much-needed book that will help equip the local church for effective disaster response. It is full of practical and helpful examples, tools and resources. One of the unique features of this book is that it is not just based on years of the authors' experience, but it is also based on the authors' research. This is a highly recommended book for clergy, church leaders and lay leaders alike."
Harold G. Koenig, MD, professor of psychiatry and behavioral sciences, Duke University Medical Center

"In this book, Drs. Jamie Aten and David Boan prepare local churches for ministering to communities impacted by disasters. Drawing on personal stories and examples from their work around the globe, they show how churches can address both the spiritual and practical needs of disaster survivors. They offer guidance on how the church can be a vehicle for justice at what are often unjust times."
The Rev. Canon Leslie J. Francis, professor of religions and education, University of Warwick

"Drs. Jamie Aten and David Boan provide an essential, preparatory wake-up call to the church in the *Disaster Ministry Handbook.* The research is clear—the church has not provided the right kind of assistance to older and disabled members and their caregivers before, during and after catastrophic events. Having led faith-based, post-Katrina and F4 tornado initiatives, I can say with confidence that lives will be saved when the guidelines of this critical book are implemented by churches and taught in seminaries."
Dr. Michael Parker, professor, University of Alabama, Center for Mental Health & Aging, associate professor, UAB Comprehensive Center for Aging

"Since the devastating Great East Japan Earthquake and tsunami disaster, churches in Japan have been learning disaster ministry in a hard way. As the general secretary of Japan Evangelical Association, there were many times I wished that I had a guidebook for this kind of ministry. This handbook by Dr. Boan and Dr. Aten clearly outlines the scope and necessary components of disaster ministry in a comprehensive manner, which gives us a big picture of what disaster ministry is all about. It also provides very practical tips and procedures that help us to put things in action and actually get things done in a real disaster situation. I have personally worked closely with Dr. Boan and Dr. Aten in our disaster response ministries in Japan and their research and insights have helped us a great deal. I would like to recommend this book for all who are involved in disaster ministry."

Kenichi Shinagawa, general secretary, Japan Evangelical Association

"This book will help you and your church prepare for possible disasters that could affect your community, and equally as important, this resource will give insight to ministry responses that can follow. I was a pastor just nine miles from the Gulf when Katrina devastated our area, and my first thoughts were, *Disaster response isn't why I'm here; God will surely call me somewhere else.* Instead, our experience brought discovery that the crisis was a unique opportunity for our church to minister to the rebuilding needs of people both physically and spiritually. This book is a must for churches to learn what they can do before and after a disaster. As a local church, you are uniquely positioned. What would it be like to be ready to respond to a crisis in your community in relevant ways as the hands and feet of Jesus?"

Nelson Roth, cofounder, Relevant Ministry, Inc., author of *Nehemiah Response*

"The authors are to be commended for producing an excellent handbook that is a prerequisite for Christian communities wanting to respond to the vulnerable in disasters. Based on thorough research and practical experience, the authors show us that sympathy and goodwill are not enough to ensure a disaster response will be truly compassionate, hold up to ethical and financial scrutiny, or be effective. Sympathy, goodwill, especially infused with godly spirituality, are necessary, but so also are thorough examination of motives and 'calling,' planning and training. This work excels in bringing all of these together to provide a treasure chest of guidance and tools that will assist churches and groups to assess both their skills and limitations for disaster response, and to plan thoroughly and train effectively. The vulnerable of their own faith communities and the civic communities they seek to serve will be all the richer for the kind of insights and practical directions this work so helpfully provides."

Roger Abbott, research associate in natural disasters, The Faraday Institute, University of Cambridge, lecturer in pastoral response to trauma, Wales Evangelical School of Theology

DISASTER MINISTRY HANDBOOK

Jamie D. Aten and David M. Boan

IVP Books

An imprint of InterVarsity Press
Downers Grove, Illinois

InterVarsity Press
P.O. Box 1400, Downers Grove, IL 60515-1426
ivpress.com
email@ivpress.com

InterVarsity Press® is the book-publishing division of InterVarsity Christian Fellowship/USA®, a movement of students and faculty active on campus at hundreds of universities, colleges and schools of nursing in the United States of America, and a member movement of the International Fellowship of Evangelical Students. For information about local and regional activities, visit intervarsity.org.

All Scripture quotations, unless otherwise indicated, are taken from THE HOLY BIBLE, NEW INTERNATIONAL VERSION®, NIV® Copyright © 1973, 1978, 1984, 2011 by Biblica, Inc.™ Used by permission. All rights reserved worldwide.

While any stories in this book are true, some names and identifying information may have been changed to protect the privacy of individuals.

Cover design: Cindy Kiple
Interior design: Beth McGill
Images: Stack of blankets: © zxcynosure/iStockphoto
       Stack of sandbags: © UncleScrooge/iStockphoto
       Wrap bandage: © herreid/iStockphoto
       Bible: © boblin/iStockphoto
       Disaster relief package: © Pamela Moore/iStockphoto

ISBN 978-0-8308-4122-6 (print)
ISBN 978-0-8308-9768-1 (digital)

Printed in the United States of America ∞

 As a member of the Green Press Initiative, InterVarsity Press is committed to protecting the environment and to the responsible use of natural resources. To learn more, visit greenpressinitiative.org.

Library of Congress Cataloging-in-Publication Data

Aten, Jamie D.
  Disaster ministry handbook / Jamie D. Aten and David M. Boan.
    pages cm
  Includes bibliographical references and index.
  ISBN 978-0-8308-4122-6 (pbk. : alk. paper)—ISBN 978-0-8308-9768-1 (ebook)
  1. Church work with disaster victims. I. Title.
  HV554.4.A84 2015
                                                    2015010652

P 27 26 25 24 23 22 21 20 19 18 17 16 15 14 13 12 11 10 9 8 7 6 5 4 3

Y 39 38 37 36 35 34 33 32 31 30 29 28 27 26 25 24 23 22 21 20

To my daughters—Colleen, Chloe and Carlee—
I am so thankful that each of you are in my life. You are each
"fearfully and wonderfully made" (Ps 139:14). It is a blessing
to watch how God continues to grow and uniquely
shape you. I love each of you dearly.

Jamie

I would like to acknowledge my dear wife Andrea's support
and encouragement when it comes to my writing. She always reminds
me that I have some things worth saying and that people would care to hear.
Some days I need to be reminded of that. I also want to express my
appreciation of my colleague Jamie, who had the vision for this
project and got the ball rolling. He continues to be
a great coworker, besides being the most
productive writer I know.

David

Contents

Part One

Foundations

chapter one

Introduction

My wife, young daughter and I (Jamie) moved from the Chicago area to South Mississippi just six days before Hurricane Katrina struck the Gulf Coast. We did not have phone service or a decent television signal, so we were unaware of the ever so rapidly and dangerously increasing storm that was headed our way. We attended a large church just down the road from our home. After the warm welcome and greetings that followed the bellowing choir's opening praise song, the pastor walked solemnly to the podium. With his jaw set, and in a slow southern drawl, he began his message by saying, "If you remember Camille, you know what I'm about to say." My wife looked at me and asked, "Who is Camille?" to which I replied jokingly, "She must be in the Old Testament." Unfortunately, we quickly learned about Hurricane Camille (which hit the Gulf Coast almost thirty years earlier) and were soon introduced to her counterpart—one of the worst natural disasters to ever strike our nation—Hurricane Katrina.

Being new to the area, as soon as the service ended I began nervously introducing myself to those in the pews around us. I wanted to know if this was something to be worried about. How do you prepare for a hurricane? I was from the North. I had never worried about hurricanes before. To my questions, I received answers like, "At worst, it's going to be like camping for a day or two," or, "You know, every year those news folks get up and tell us to take cover and get everyone upset, and for nothing, 'cause nothing happens. So I wouldn't worry too much about it." Despite their trying to reassure us, something did not feel right. So from church my family and I drove to my work office for Internet access. In my mind's eye I can still see my wife sitting at my desk, pulling up the national weather station live radar while my daughter sat on my lap. Looking at the radar on the screen, I thought, *We must be zoomed in on the image*, but we were not. I had never seen anything like this before. From my office we headed home to try and get ready for the fast-approaching storm.

I soon found myself standing in our living room thinking and trying to remember all the things I had ever heard about preparedness and disasters. I recalled being an elementary child sitting under my desk with my hands over my head and my head between my knees. *Okay, so that's not going to help*, I thought to myself. *Think, Jamie. Just think. What else have you learned?* Then I remembered all those post-9/11 public service ads that seemed to be everywhere at the time. So I ran to the kitchen and pulled open the junk drawer (you know, the one with twenty pens that don't work and everything else you do not know what to do with). Eureka! I found it. *I am ready*, I thought to myself. I reached into the back of the drawer and pulled out a brand-new roll of duct tape. I quickly made my way through the house, duct tape in hand. I remembered that almost everything I had watched, read or heard about preparedness after 9/11 said, "Have duct tape."

There I was, standing in the middle of the living room looking out our window knowing a threat was rapidly approaching. And all I could think was, *Now what?* Though I had a resource that was supposedly able to help me, I had no idea what to do with it.

My story is not unique. Most people do not know how to effectively prepare for or respond to disasters. Moreover, in conducting research around the globe, David and I have found a great deal of variability among how ready churches are for disasters. Some churches in high-risk areas are relatively prepared, and others little or not at all. We have found an alarming trend: most churches realize there are threats but few do anything ahead of time to actually prepare for disasters. Though we have found many churches volunteer and help other churches in communities that are affected by disasters, most are not ready for a disaster that could directly impact their congregation or community. However, there is good news. There are numerous practical steps congregations can take to prepare for and recover from disasters.

Purpose

Thus, the purpose of this book is to help churches learn how to plan, launch and sustain disaster ministries. Throughout this handbook we will provide best practices and lessons learned that will help your church and community to be more resilient in the face of catastrophes, crises and emergencies. David and I (Jamie) will also share numerous examples throughout the book to help you apply what you are learning. Many will come from my own personal Hurricane Katrina experience and from my time living in Mississippi. We will also provide examples from the work that David and I have done through Wheaton College's Humanitarian Disaster Institute (HDI) all over the world with churches impacted by disasters and humanitarian crises. Then we will introduce discussion questions and tools that will help you and your congregation build on this knowledge so that you can develop an effective disaster ministry. Overall, this handbook is designed to help you navigate disasters, from emergency planning through the recovery process. The handbook gives congregations and denominations or associations the critical concepts and components of effective emergency planning and response.

Why This Handbook

Since the 1980s there has been roughly a 400 percent increase in natural disasters.[1] The world's five costliest natural disasters have occurred in the past twenty years, with three of those disasters striking in the last eight years alone. There have also been nearly 5,000 terrorist events annually over the last ten years.[2] As we write in HDI's *Ready Faith: Planning Guide,*

> Natural disasters such as floods, earthquakes, fires and tornadoes can strike a community with little or no warning. An influenza pandemic, or other infectious disease, can spread from person to person causing serious illness across the country or around the globe in a very short time. Mass shootings have increased in frequency. The harrowing events of September 11 and subsequent terrorist attempts have ushered in a new awareness of terrorist threats. The unfortunate reality is that many congregations in this country may be touched either directly or indirectly by a disaster of some kind at any time.[3]

In brief, you might think of a disaster as anything that disrupts civic society. (See next chapter for more in-depth description and definitions.)

In our research[4] and the research of others,[5] it has been found that many people turn to faith and to local congregations for answers and assistance when disaster strikes. You may have never thought about your church's role in responding to a disaster in your own community. But if your doors are open after a disaster strikes your area, people will come to you for help.[6] "Knowing what to do when faced with a crisis can be the difference between calm and chaos, between courage and fear, between life and death."[7] If you are going to be ready, the time to plan is now. When a crisis strikes, it is too late to get prepared and too late to start working with those in need. By taking action now you can save lives and prevent harm during a disaster as you extend your ministry to those who need help.

Another reason you should read this handbook is because it will help your church respond to our biblical calling to justice. In the most basic view, this is a book about justice. We will make the case that the vulnerable suffer disproportionately from all types of disasters. Further, the vulnerable often go unrecognized as vulnerable, or for a host of reasons are not helped by many public programs. This is a place where the church belongs and needs to be present. You may have heard it said that "disasters don't discriminate." There is some truth to this, that regardless of financial status, race, ethnicity, gender and so on, disasters can impact anyone. However, the longer that we have been doing this research, the more our eyes have been opened to how disasters reveal injustices. The poor, fragile, very old and young, people with the fewest resources and connections are actually at more risk and have a more difficult time recovering than others. Therein lies an opportunity for the church, as well as one of the basic reasons we wrote this handbook.

Who Should Read This Handbook

On a practical level, the handbook is for anyone who is part of or works with congregations and has a heart for disaster ministry—whether a pastor, lay leader, professional in relief and development, or academic researcher. The material is designed to speak to the questions and issues that congregations face when they consider a disaster ministry. The material in this handbook does not require or assume any particular set of skills or knowledge. All that is needed is a desire to help others and a prayerful attitude.

Why Congregations Should Have a Disaster Ministry

Churches see serving those in need as a basic expression of Christ's love. When disaster strikes a community, near or far, church members want to do something to express their concern and care. Add to that the fact that disasters are on the rise, and you see a rapidly growing number of disaster ministries. Further, as population density increases, the potential impact of disasters in terms of the human toll drastically increases. At the same time, government resources are facing cuts and there is a growing recognition that government certainly cannot do it all, and cannot do it alone. For all these reasons, congregations have an opportunity to become involved in disasters as a basic area of ministry. We have heard the following from congregation leaders who support a disaster ministry:

- Congregations can provide broad-based prevention as well as holistic care for individuals after a disaster incident. Holistic care provides for the physical, emotional and spiritual parts of a person's life.

- Congregations can reach people in need that other groups and agencies cannot reach, and thus help those who would otherwise go unserved.

- Disaster work can be integrated into the other ministries of a congregation and strengthen those same ministries.

- Congregations can be a source for community action. The connection with people in the community helps with assessing needs and risks and identifying possible actions.

- Congregations can advocate on behalf of the marginalized and vulnerable, as in ensuring fair distributions of health care or food, or determining where help is needed most.

- Congregations may provide key resources during a disaster, such as using a meeting space as a rest or evacuation center, or storing and distributing food, water, equipment and other resources.

- Congregations are already a center for communication, allowing meetings and messages to be communicated to a significant number of people on a regular basis.

- Congregations can provide a willing body of volunteers (members of the congregation, clergy and leaders) who are motivated by love and compassion.[8]

There are also scriptural and theological reasons to be concerned about disasters, though it may not be in the way you may think. A basic premise of our work is that disasters reveal the underlying fabric of a community. As we have stated, vulnerable people suffer disproportionately in a disaster. Further, the ways of being vulnerable to a disaster are greater than most people realize. Vulnerability comes from a wide variety of characteristics, such as being a single parent with young children (anyone who has parented multiple young children knows that everything related to running a home is more complicated), being medically fragile, very young, very old, or poor. Even the type of job you have can increase vulnerability. In my work, I can do my job from anywhere, as long as I have a computer and a phone (which I generally carry with me). If I was a machinist and the machine shop was destroyed in a disaster, I would be out of work for an unknown length of time. The same is true for any job dependent upon equipment or a facility, like a restaurant or office building.

Therefore, we restate the question from "Should churches be involved in disasters?" to "Should churches be serving those most vulnerable to harm?" The disaster event, then, is not the focus of ministry; it is the test of how well the community cares for those who are most vulnerable.[9] Put that way, the scriptural support is clear and well known to most Christians, from the proclamation of the church as the salt of the earth, the call to the church as the light of the world (Mt 5:13-16) and the repeated call throughout the Bible to serve the vulnerable (e.g., Mt 25:35; Acts 10:4).

Strengths of the Local Congregation

Disasters are not only a test of the community and the church, but they are also opportunities for the church to show its strengths. Local congregations are uniquely situated in their communities to help with disaster preparedness, response and recovery. This position is due to the character of the church as a community of service that cares for one another and the community around them, bearing witness to the work of Christ through their relationships. This character serves as the basis for establishing relationships of trust based on wanting what is best for the other person. This trust means the church has, or can have, relationships with people that agencies or outside groups cannot have. To understand how important and special this is, consider the disaster examples we listed at the start. Immigrant workers often live in fear of deportation, so they do not ask for help and certainly do not talk to government agencies. Elderly people in high-crime areas live in fear of being harmed and may not open their doors to people they do not know, even if those people are trying to help them survive a heat wave. The elderly are especially vulnerable during natural disasters because they may not know what to do, or they may need help to move but do not know where to find that help. Each of these cases requires a relationship of trust built up over time so that the needs of these vulnerable groups are known and someone can minister to them. No group or agency is in the position to connect with people and build trust the way the local church is.

Besides building relationships of trust, the local church is often faithful in serving the community, staying for the long term. People see this in the way the local church is often first to respond and last to leave in a disaster. Because it is part of the community, it has a long-term presence that allows people to trust that it will be there when needed. The local church is most likely to know where the needs are and how to serve them. For example, a local emergency management office we frequently work with found that although they wanted to send people to the most vulnerable during a disaster, such as the elderly or medically fragile, their database of where these people lived was often out of date. As a result, valuable time was wasted sending emergency workers to locations where no one lived. Their solution to the problem was to work with local churches to reach out to people in need as they were the ones most likely to know the neighborhoods.

Handbook Development

Much of the information in this handbook draws on the experiences and wisdom of the overall Christian relief community. In the following pages we unpack what we have learned from some of the great resources available. We have also adapted promising practices from the broader emergency-management community that can be used to help your congregation. Further, we share heavily out of our own experiences of helping and studying disasters around the globe:

- Hurricanes Katrina, Rita and Gustav

- the national H1N1 outbreak

- the 2010 Mississippi Delta and 2011 Tuscaloosa tornadoes

- the Haiti earthquake and Japan earthquake and tsunami

- Deepwater Horizon oil spill

- typhoons in the Philippines

- displaced people in Kenya and the Democratic Republic of the Congo

The recommendations we make are also based on our work with churches of all sizes, types and denominations; Christian relief and development organizations; public health departments; and emergency management agencies.[10]

Handbook Organization

The general structure of our handbook largely revolves around some of the specific stages of disaster (see more in the next chapter), providing instruction on how congregations might take action before, in the midst of and after a disaster. In working with churches we have found this three-stage approach to be a practical and helpful way for getting started. We are not alone in taking this approach. In fact, this is the strategy most government agencies and Christian organizations involved in emergency response have recommended (and use in their respective resources) for developing high-quality emergency plans.[11]

You will find that each chapter has numerous tools, resources and discussion questions to help you with the tasks described. Overall, we encourage readers to take a developmental approach to applying these materials to their congregation. That is, start small and build up your congregation's capacity to prepare for and respond to disasters over time. In such an approach, the objective is accomplished as foundations are placed and then built up over time. Throughout the handbook, we aim to walk alongside you as a mentor would, pointing you in the direction of actions that will help your congregation develop greater resilience to disasters.

Keep in mind that as with any book we could not cover everything. We encourage you to check out some of the references we cite throughout the book to dig even deeper into ways your church might serve amid disasters.

This handbook focuses on preparing your own congregation with both general plans that can be incorporated into other ministries and specialized plans for the disasters you are most likely to face in your area. In the pages that follow we will introduce you to a different way to think about disasters, not only as the occasional crisis that may strike your church but also as a test that reveals the nature of the community. This view of disasters calls upon the church to do what it does best: care for the weak, the poor and the vulnerable; get involved in the community; seek out those in need; and approach disaster preparedness as a ministry that cuts across everything the church does.

In this introductory chapter, our goal has been to orient you to the need and reasons to engage in disaster ministry. In our opening remarks we have also sought to introduce you to the strengths of the local church in disaster contexts and to provide a general overview of the structure of the book and how it was developed.

In chapter two, "Disaster Basics," we provide a basic understanding of disasters to help better prepare you and your congregation for disasters by making you more aware of potential threats and ways

to reduce those threats. Familiarizing yourself with this material will provide important information you can use and share with others to boost your congregation's and community's ability to recover after a disaster. Further, the material covered in this chapter will help you better tailor your congregation's disaster ministry toward the unique challenges or threats you may encounter.

In chapter three, "Disasters, Justice and the Church," we further explore the role of the church in disasters and encourage you to think about how to help the most vulnerable in your congregation and community. There are several reasons that we have devoted an entire chapter to this issue: first, we believe justice is a biblical mandate for the church to follow, and second, we argue that creating a general disaster ministry focusing on who is vulnerable (along with specialized preparation) will help you be prepared for all forms of disasters and more.

In chapter four, "Getting Started," we present the various ways different congregations have approached disaster ministry, the types of programs they started and how they began. There is no one approach that fits everyone. Our hope for this chapter is that you will see an approach that works for your congregation and come away with some concrete strategies for launching a disaster ministry.

In chapter five, "Planning," we will help you identify areas of concern and establish a plan for your congregation and your family, which will lay the foundation for successful preparedness. Disaster ministry plans need to address a range of events and emergencies caused both by nature and by people, including all-hazards (i.e., any incident, natural or human caused, that requires an organized response) and public health emergencies. As a result, planning may seem overwhelming. However, we want to reassure you that though it takes time and effort, it is manageable. Thus, in this chapter we will help you learn to do the following:

1. conduct a disaster risk assessment for your congregation and community

2. engage leadership in developing a disaster ministry vision and goals

3. develop a continuity of ministry and operations plan (COMOP)

4. test and practice your plan

In chapter six, "Response," we walk you through a critical series of common response actions that you and your congregation may be called upon to carry out in the immediate aftermath of a disaster. Specifically, we focus on four things:

1. how to implement your plan

2. evacuation and sheltering

3. crisis communication

4. protecting property

In chapter seven, "Recovery," we discuss how to prepare your disaster ministry for helping your congregation and community rebound from disaster over the long haul. In this chapter we will cover common recovery activities, as well as strategies for how your church can help other congregations and churches. The goal of the recovery phase is to help people rebuild and start to put their lives back together. Con-

centrate on the congregants, community members and facilities, and don't worry about how much time recovery is taking.

In chapter eight, "Providing Basic Disaster Spiritual and Emotional Care," we introduce you to a wide range of interpersonal helping strategies. We have devoted an entire chapter to this subject because we believe it cuts across all disaster ministry activities. This chapter focuses on delivering supportive care while avoiding the pitfalls of giving well-intentioned but unhelpful advice. It will help you recognize what is (and is not) healthy support. In this chapter we also offer recommendations for supporting the emotional and spiritual needs of children affected by disasters. We cover guidelines for referring survivors for additional mental health care, as well as provide strategies for recognizing and preventing burnout and secondary trauma.

In chapter nine, "Case Studies in Disaster Ministry," we introduce three in-depth case studies to further help you apply the lessons that you learned in this handbook. These case studies provide a firsthand account of how other church leaders and congregations have prepared for and responded to disasters. Specifically, we highlight cases from the Philippines, Japan and the United States, and then bring attention to common themes that emerge across cases.

In chapter ten, "Conclusion," we review the major lessons and take-home ideas, skills and recommendations covered in the earlier chapters. We also offer some of our thoughts about the best ways to get started and sustain your disaster ministry. Finally, we issue a challenge for those starting a disaster ministry to do so with the vulnerable in mind.

Conclusion

In this book we will equip you with much more than duct tape. Overall, the aim of this handbook is to help your congregation establish an effective disaster ministry. Our hope is that it will stimulate thinking about the role and ministry of the church within a disaster context. Further, we hope that this book will provide you with lots of helpful and practical information, tools and resources for developing and sustaining your congregation's disaster ministry. By taking action now you can save lives and prevent harm during a disaster and expand your ministry.

Discussion Questions

1. Where does your church fall on the spectrum of preparedness? Do you already have an active disaster ministry or is this all brand-new to you?

2. Why are you personally interested in starting a disaster ministry?

3. What do you see as your congregation's greatest strengths? How might you build on these strengths as you begin the steps toward starting a disaster ministry?

chapter two

Disaster Basics

Few people—let alone churches—were prepared for the H1N1 outbreak of 2009. This was entirely different from what most people think of when they hear the word *disaster*. It did not destroy homes. It did not leave a path of physical destruction. Rather, it was a public health emergency (more on that later in the chapter). What initially presented as symptoms similar to the common flu (e.g., fever, body aches) would turn quickly into a much more intense set of problems, and in some occasions death.[1] With a hurricane you often have weeks to see the storm forming and the path it is taking. You can see it coming. This pandemic was largely invisible other than the symptoms displayed by the host. In most cases it was spread by insect bites or human contact.[2] This threat was unlike any recent disaster in our country's history. Because of Katrina, people living in Mississippi had a better idea of what to expect and how to respond to extreme weather events. However, the region was not ready for this outbreak, and the disease rapidly spread throughout the state.

A few months after the outbreak, a local public health department and a local min-istry association contacted me to consult with them. The churches belonging to this ministerial association noticed that H1N1 appeared to be spreading through their congregations at a pace more rapid than other community groups and organizations were experiencing. I (Jamie) was asked to spend some time studying and consulting with them to help them figure out why H1N1 seemed to be having such an impact on their churches.

After Katrina the churches learned the power of cooperating—that it was imperative to work together when faced with a disaster. So as the H1N1 pandemic began to intensify, many churches did just that: they held public meetings, they sent volunteers to care for the sick, and they came together to support one another. This worked for the churches when responding to extreme weather events, but it seemed to be having the opposite effect this time. As I met with this group of public health and church leaders, I asked them to first share what they knew about H1N1. I discovered a lot of misinformation about the pandemic. Once this misinformation was addressed, I went on to ask them to walk me through from start to finish the typical Sunday morning routine the average congregation member might have at their churches. I asked them to give me as much detail as possible, as though I were watching a videotape.

Their descriptions went something like this. Most members' first experience was shaking hands with or hugging a greeter or greeters at the entryway of the church. If it was a chilly morning, people might hang up their jackets in the coatroom. This might be followed by worship in the sanctuary, then a brief period of greeting people around them. People would then sign the register with the paper and pencil provided and pass it down the aisle for the rest of the people in the pew to sign. After the sermon, it was common for the members to pass the communion plates, or depending on the tradition, to take communion from the same goblet and from the same loaf of bread. Next came the passing of the offering plates. Finally there might be more songs, then the final prayer and blessing. People would then make their goodbyes or perhaps join together for a potluck lunch.

All of what they described are common ways most churches worship together or represent liturgy or common religious practices. Unfortunately, the way many of these rituals were conducted accounted for the sharp spike in H1N1 among these churches' membership. People were spreading H1N1 as they shook hands, as they passed an item down the pew, and so on and so on. The common practices of these churches and the common ways they had acted to help them cope with previous disasters were actually making them sick. After I pointed

this out, one of the public health officials' first reaction was that the churches should stop meeting, or at least stop things like taking communion. As you can imagine, this did not go over well with the clergy.

At this point I asked if there might be other ways to help curb the increase. Examples of ideas shared in that meeting probably mirror strategies that you heard after the outbreak, like making disinfectant hand sanitizer readily available (such as when entering the church, before taking communion, etc.), encouraging people to cough into their elbow and instructing members to stay home if they had flu-like symptoms. Making some relatively easy changes to the common routines of these churches helped drastically slow down the spread of H1N1 in local congregations and allowed them to keep meeting. This example demonstrates that not all disasters are alike, and different disasters require different responses.

Purpose

In this chapter we provide a basic understanding of disaster types and stages. This will help better prepare you and your congregation for disasters by making you more aware of a wide range of potential threats. Familiarizing yourself with this material will provide crucial information you can use and share with others to strengthen your congregation's and community's ability to tailor responses to the unique challenges of these different types of disasters.[3]

Disasters Defined

The Oklahoma Medical Reserve Corps website offers the following helpful overview:

By definition, a disaster is "an occurrence causing widespread destruction and distress, a grave misfortune, a total failure. . . ." A disaster is often further defined as being either a man-made or natural event that results in death, injury, and property damage which cannot be managed through normal, routine channels. A disaster requires immediate and effective intervention of multiple government and private sector organizations to help meet the needs of the community and area just after the disaster occurs and the area and people begin to recover.[4]

Types of Disasters

Disasters vary in their range, scope and intensity from incidents that directly or indirectly touch a lone community to an entire region to the whole nation (e.g., September 11). Remember that an incident in another city or state can still affect a given congregation or locality. For example, a disaster in another community can send survivors to your community for assistance. Identifying an approaching threat and knowing how to protect yourself, your family, your congregation and your community will aid you in both preparation beforehand and recovery afterward.

Natural disasters. Natural disasters such as floods, fires, earthquakes, tornadoes and windstorms affect thousands of people every year. Other types of natural disasters may be common in your location—wildfires in the western part of the United States; heat waves in some cities, especially affecting the elderly and medically fragile; fog in parts of California and Texas, leading to

multicar pileups on freeways. Write down possible disaster threats for your area. Examples include:

- Earthquake
- Tornado
- Hurricane
- Landslide, mudslide, subsidence
- Flood, flash flood, tidal surge
- Water control structure, dam or levee failure
- Drought
- Snow, ice, hail, sleet, arctic freeze
- Windstorm
- Tropical cyclone
- Volcanic eruption
- Tsunami
- Extreme temperatures (heat or cold)
- Lightning strikes (wildfire following)
- Pandemic, infectious or communicable disease (e.g., avian flu, H1N1)[5]

Technological and accidental hazards. Because of the increasing number of new substances, the intricacy of systems, and opportunities for human error with these materials, the potential for accidental disasters is rising. These disasters often come with little or no warning. Examples of technological and accidental hazards include:

- Hazardous material spill or release (e.g., oil spill)
- Utility interruption or failure
- Nuclear power plant incident
- Explosion or fire

- Transportation accident (e.g., motor vehicle, railroad, watercraft, aircraft, pipeline)

- Building or structure collapse (e.g., coal mine accident)

Terrorist hazards. Across the history of civilization, there have been many hazards to the security of nations. These hazards have resulted in death, property destruction, extensive illness and injury, the eviction of many groups of people, and catastrophic economic consequences. Technological breakthroughs and continuous political unrest have also threatened national security. As we write in HDI's *Ready Faith: Planning Guide*, "There is a tendency to think of terrorism as something that the government handles and not something people plan for. However, if your congregation is sending mission teams into certain developing areas, such as Haiti or parts of Africa, you may be more at risk than you realize. As you assess your risks and things you must plan for, remember your missions and service teams that could be putting themselves at risk."[6] Examples of terrorist hazards include:

- Kidnapping, extortion

- Civil disturbance

- Hostage incident

- Bombing or bomb threat

- Workplace violence

Public health emergencies. Though most people reading this handbook are familiar with the disasters covered above, few congregations are as aware of or as prepared to address public health emergencies. *Bio-terrorism hazards* represent one potential public health emergency that congregations should be familiar with. An attack is considered bioterrorism when germs, bacteria or viruses are purposely released to cause harm, usually resulting in death or illness of humans or animals. Due to globalization and the ease of transference via individuals, water, air and food, bioterrorist attacks are difficult to detect until they have affected large groups of people. *Biological hazards* represent another example of a public health emergency. These include deadly or injurious germs, bacteria or viruses. The number of potential outbreaks is escalating due to the new forms of viruses, the speed at which they spread and the difficulty of creating new and effective medications. Diseases can be contracted through ingestion, physical contact and inhalation.[7]

Other public health emergencies, such as pandemic flu, communicable diseases and food-borne illnesses, can also strike a community with little or no warning. An infectious disease such as influenza can be easily and rapidly transmitted, leading to serious disorder in a country or across the globe. Flu outbreaks can be deadly for some vulnerable people, and they have increased in frequency. Like all hazards, public health emergencies can also be classified into different categories. Below are examples of the most common public health emergency classifications.

Pandemic flu. Pandemic flu (or influenza) is a respiratory virus that is carried from person to person through coughing and sneezing. It can lead to mild to severe illness and even death. The best way to protect yourself and your family is to get vaccinated. Examples of the virus include influenza A (H1N1) and influenza B.

Communicable diseases. Communicable diseases are infectious diseases that spread from person to person or from animals to people. Examples include E. coli, salmonella and H1N1. The Centers for Disease Control and Prevention estimated the H1N1 flu was responsible for between 8,870 and 18,300 deaths.[8] This is one example of the unfortunate fact that many congregations in this country may be touched, directly or indirectly, by a public health emergency of some kind, which can occur at any time.

Aside from pandemics, many people are unaware of the threat of the annual flu. The CDC estimates the annual mortality from the flu ranges between 3,000 and 49,000, depending on the strain of the flu virus.[9] Most of the victims are either very old, very young or have other health risks that make them more vulnerable. Caring for those at risk need not wait for the next pandemic.

Food-borne/waterborne illnesses. Food-borne illness (or "food poisoning") is a common yet preventable public health problem. Each year one in six Americans gets sick by consuming contaminated foods or beverages. There are many disease-causing microbes, pathogens, chemicals and other harmful substances that can cause food-borne disease, including salmonella and staphylococcus.[10]

Disaster Classifications

Disasters are classified according to several dimensions. We have a tendency to lump all disasters into the same category, but di-saters vary in complexity and impact. Therefore, it is helpful to understand some of the differences between various classifications of disasters.

Extent of destruction. Beyond the area affected, the time span of the episode and restoration contribute to classifying disasters as local, widespread or catastrophic. A home fire can be as devastating to the victims as a monumental hurricane. The extent of destruction can also vary greatly, as well as the type of disruptions that may occur to a community from disaster type to disaster type. For example, when we hear the word *disasters* we most frequently think of *high-visibility disasters*, which are like hurricanes or tsunamis where the damage is often immediate and often generates a lot of media coverage. Unless record setting, other disasters like droughts or heat waves are considered *low-visibility disasters* because they sometimes fly under the radar of the media and may not generate as much attention as other forms of disasters.

Primary and secondary disasters. A primary disaster is the initial or triggering event. A secondary disaster is an effect of the first event. For example, earthquakes, tornadoes, floods and fires are generally primary disasters. Any of these first events can trigger secondary disasters. An earthquake can lead to a power failure, dam failure, tidal wave or fire. Tornadoes frequently result in power outages. Floods and fires can cause a ripple effect of destruction. As we were writing this, an estimated 5,200 people died when Typhoon Haiyan hit the Philippines. Another 2,800 died in the days following from the secondary mudslides and flooding caused by the typhoon.

Natural and manmade disasters. Natural disasters include tornadoes, hurricanes, drought, snow and ice—any hazard due to weather conditions—as well as volcanic eruptions and earthquakes. Manmade disasters can have major consequences as well. These include fires, riots, explosions, transportation accidents, terrorist attacks and war.

Disaster Phases

There is great variance in the amount of notice a community receives before a disaster. Earthquakes, for example, generally come with no warning. Floods and hurricanes provide hours or days to gird up. The amount of time before a disaster affects how victims respond. As one manual puts it, "When there is no warning, survivors may feel vulnerable, unsafe and fearful of future unpredicted tragedies. The perception that they had no control over protecting themselves or their loved ones can be deeply distressing. When people do not heed warnings and suffer losses as a result, they may experience guilt and self-blame. While they may have specific plans for how they might protect themselves in the future, they can be left with a sense of guilt or responsibility for what has occurred."[11]

Impact phase. This phase ranges from wild and unpredictable (for example, tornadoes and explosions) to a slow and steady buildup (for example, some types of floods). The extent of the psychological and social effects will correspond to the breadth and personal costs of the disaster. People's reactions will vary, ranging from "constricted, stunned, shock-like responses to the less common overt expressions of panic or hysteria."[12] People generally react first with bewilderment and disbelief, and their emphasis is on the survival and status of themselves and their friends and family. When members of a family are in different locations during the event itself, they will be anxious to reconcile.

Heroic phase. Directly following a disaster, survival, rescue and safety are para-

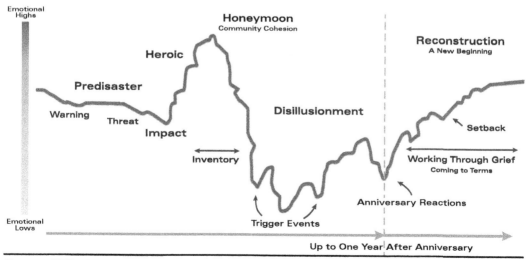

Figure 2.1. FEMA's Phases of Disaster: Collective Reactions

mount, and sometimes evacuation is necessary. Some people experience postimpact disorientation as adrenaline-driven actions to save lives and property. Yet this phase deserves a cautionary note: "While activity level may be high, actual productivity is often low. The capacity to assess risk may be impaired and injuries can result."[13] The heroic phase is also associated with altruism in both survivors and emergency responders. Posttrauma reactions also often occur at this time, particularly when there are physical risks or when families are separated during evacuation. Concern for the well-being of loved ones who are not present can hinder the focus needed for problem solving in the moment.

Honeymoon phase. This phase covers the week to months after a disaster. In this stretch, formal government and volunteer assistance may be easily accessible. Communities feel close and united due to the experience of the calamity and the support available after. Survivors can feel uplifted, confident that the aid they will receive can restore them. If mental health workers are present and viewed as valuable, they can be more easily received and can build a foundation for the phases to follow.

Disillusionment phase. In this phase the survivors' bubble is burst as they come to realize that disaster assistance is limited. Physical exhaustion builds up as a result of heavy burdens, including financial struggles and geographical displacement. The idealism of the honeymoon phase yields to dejection and weariness. The scaling down of assistance agencies and volunteer groups present can lead survivors to feel forsaken and bitter. The

chasm between assistance received and the resources needed to return to predisaster "normal" becomes clear, and troubles proliferate: "Family discord, financial losses, bureaucratic hassles, time constraints, home reconstruction, relocation and lack of recreation or leisure time." Further, "health problems and exacerbations of pre-existing conditions emerge due to ongoing, unrelenting stress and fatigue."[14] Those less affected by the disaster may be moving on, leading to hostility and disappointment for survivors, and survivors may be bitter among themselves as varying monetary amounts are distributed. This perceived inequality impairs community bonds.

Disillusionment and civil unrest can also follow when people learn that there was human influence in what first appeared to be a natural disaster (i.e., an act of God turns out to have been an act of man). For example, researchers Nel and Righarts explored how often civil unrest is linked to natural disasters.[15] They found a strong connection between disasters and civil unrest, especially among the poor in developed countries and generally among underdeveloped countries. One implication is that the poor see the disaster as exposing the injustice that already exists in their community and that put them in harm's way. We will explore this idea, and the implications for the church, in the next chapter.

Reconstruction phase. This stage, consisting of the reconstruction of property and the restoration of emotional health, can extend for years. At this point "survivors have realized that they will need to solve the problems of rebuilding their own homes, businesses, and lives largely by themselves and have gradually assumed the responsibility for doing so."[16] Yet with the remodeling of homes and communities another stage of loss arrives, as survivors must reacclimate to a new or significantly altered environment as they go on grieving. By this point family and friends may have grown tired of providing support, and other emotional resources may have dried up. The end of this stage is acceptance: "When people come to see meaning, personal growth, and opportunity from their disaster experience despite their losses and pain, they are well on the road to recovery."[17] Disasters are often accompanied by deep and transformative losses, but they also come with the opportunity to identify character strengths and reprioritize one's life.

Progression through these stages will vary among both individuals and communities, tied to the nature of the disaster and the level of involvement. The steps toward recovery may not always be as orderly as portrayed here, "as each person and community brings unique elements to the recovery process."[18]

Sequence of Disaster Management

People often conceive of disasters in terms of the event that led to loss or turmoil. But in reality, work on catastrophes includes a full range of things, with the extreme acute being just one phase. Extensive interviews and an analysis of the crisis literature indicate that experts employ four phases of crisis management. As we put it in HDI's *Ready Faith: Planning Guide*:

- *Mitigation/prevention* addresses what congregations can do to reduce or eliminate risk to life and property.
- *Preparedness* focuses on the process of planning for the worst-case scenario.
- *Response* is devoted to the steps to take during a disaster.
- *Recovery* deals with how to restore ministry operations after a disaster.[19]

As should be clear, disaster planning is an ongoing process that considers all phases of disasters (see figure 2.2). Each phase is an opportunity to serve your church and community, though it is not necessary to take on every phase. For example, as we say elsewhere, "In Japan, where churches are typically small and resources limited, churches in a region join

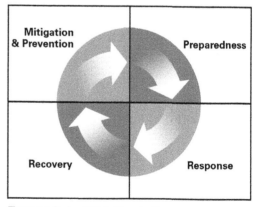

Figure 2.2 Cycle of Crisis Planning[20]

together into a church network, with each church taking a part of the overall disaster plan. The network emphasizes collaboration, resource sharing, shared training and more, with each church deciding for itself what role it will play and what resources it can contribute" over the cycle of crisis planning.[21]

Conclusion

Extreme weather gets everyone's attention, and while that is a good thing, it also leads us to think that disasters are all about extreme weather. But disasters can be caused by both nature and humans. The H1N1 outbreak of 2009 demonstrated that not all disasters are caused by natural disasters or terrorist events. An epidemic, civil conflict and climate change are also examples of disasters. Although when we hear the word *disaster* we often think of things like hurricanes and tornadoes, the church also needs to be aware of the real needs that can result from lower-profile disasters like heat waves and public health emergencies.

Discussion Questions

1. What types of disasters pose the greatest threat to your congregation and community?

2. What types of low-profile disasters are common in your community or region?

3. How might your church need to prepare differently for a public health emergency versus an extreme weather event?

4. Given the most likely disasters in your community, who is most at risk for these disasters?

chapter three

Disasters, Justice and the Church

About seven months before my family moved to Mississippi and before Hurricane Katrina, I (Jamie) had the chance to spend some time along the Mississippi Gulf Coast. I flew from O'Hare International Airport in Chicago to the Gulfport-Biloxi Airport in Gulfport, Mississippi, to interview for my first academic post. I remember having to dig and shovel my car out of the snow before heading to the airport that morning. Needless to say I was pleased when I stepped off the plane later that day to a beautiful and warm sunny day in Mississippi. I was fortunate that a future colleague was there to pick me up and take me for a drive along the coast before heading to the hotel in preparation of my interview that was to follow the next day. As we drove down the coast, I was struck by the beauty of the ocean, the cool breeze and wispy clouds on one side of the road. On the other side of the road were numerous beautiful, historical estate homes with grand colonial pillars, many with giant oak trees dating back centuries. Many of these homes were owned by affluent

families or families in which the homes had been passed down generations.

Fast-forward a little more than a month after Hurricane Katrina. I had taken a team of graduate students working with me in my research lab to the coast in Gulfport to survey people's needs in the wake of the storm. Many of the roads were blocked, destroyed or being worked on. We had to park a ways inland and navigate our way through the debris to get to the communities that lined the once scenic coastline I had taken in just months before. Most of the media coverage after Hurricane Katrina focused on New Orleans, which has left us with harrowing images of flooding. However, the damage looked significantly different along the Mississippi coast. Rather than an image of flooding, it looked like a giant bomb had gone off. Many of the beautiful homes lining the road were just gone, leaving behind slabs of concrete that made up the foundation. There were also some homes that survived by what appeared to be chance. Other homes were reduced to what looked like giant piles of matches scattered on their property. Portions of buildings were completely gutted by the force of the winds and ocean. Boats had washed up into the yards of residents, and in some cases cars in parking lots were forced into giant piles like you might see in a junkyard. Many of the century-old oak trees were damaged, some completely gone. Those that survived were filled with debris, clothes, furniture and the like.

I remember returning again to Gulfport a few months later. This time we found some of the debris gone and some homes being fixed or even rebuilt. By the end of the year, though the damage was overwhelming and in some places still looked like a war zone, you could see signs of promise and progress. Many of the large waterfront homes were being restored.

This was not the case in Forest Heights, a primarily African American neighborhood of 200 homes in Gulfport just about a mile from where we were. In the 1960s Forest Heights was developed as a model community for promoting African American homeownership.[1] Before Katrina, despite facing harsh economic challenges, many of the residents now owned their homes. On one of my visits to the coast I had a chance to interview a pastor from this community for a study I was working on. He shared that just a few years before the storm, several residents, some of whom attended his church, had a deed-burning ceremony to celebrate now being homeowners. He went on to say that many of his congregation's members who had celebrated could not believe they were actually homeowners, that this accomplishment had always seemed like a far-off dream

until it actually happened. He went on to describe how starkly different the recovery process was for his community from other more wealthy communities along the coast. Whereas there were signs of progress in more affluent neighborhoods a year after Hurricane Katrina, the rebuilding efforts in Forest Heights starkly lagged behind. Many of the residents were without insurance or were underinsured, did not have flood insurance, and were therefore unable to rebuild. As I left my interview and drove through the community, I saw a FEMA trailer in almost every yard, as well as what looked like piles—and in some cases, hills—of debris. Many of the homes I saw with significant damage appeared left untouched except for the occasional blue tarps draped across rooftops to try and prevent further water damage.

Purpose

In the opening chapter we briefly introduced the idea of vulnerability, noting that vulnerable people suffer disproportionately greater harm in a disaster compared to less vulnerable people, and that disaster ministry is a practice of restoring justice. In the present chapter, we further explore the role of the church in disasters and encourage you to think about how to help the most vulnerable in your congregation and community. There are three reasons that we have devoted an entire chapter to this issue. First, vulnerability is fundamentally an issue of justice, and we believe justice is a biblical mandate for the church to follow. Second, unless your ministry is aware of the plight of those who are vulnerable and how disaster affects them, you

Table 3.1

Types of Vulnerability	
Socioeconomic Status	Status is an important resource that allows some people to have more influence in the community, often as a way to help get their needs met. Similarly, lack of status can mean more vulnerability.
Gender	Women can be more vulnerable in several ways. They are more likely than men to have family caretaking responsibilities. They may also have lower wages and find changes in jobs to be more challenging, all of which translate into a more difficult response to a crisis.
Race and Ethnicity	Language and cultural barriers make it harder for people to understand services and know how to access them. In our part of the Midwest, immigrants and refugees are often ill prepared for severe weather, and newly arriving people often have little understanding of how to use police and fire services, or the appropriate use of 911. Barriers in a community between different ethnic groups make the community more vulnerable by limiting cooperation and support across the community.
Age	Extremes of age affect one's movement out of harm's way. The elderly and very young are most vulnerable to heat and cold because of the difficulty moderating body temperature. Anyone with multiple very young children can tell you that all activities are more complicated.
Employment	Loss of employment has long-term consequences for well-being. A disaster can lead to an economic downturn that will affect some people more severely than others.
Location	Rural residents are more vulnerable because of having fewer services and having to contend with greater distances to access services.
Residence	Some homes are more easily destroyed (e.g., mobile homes) while others may not be up to building codes. In some parts of the world, construction in poor areas may not meet building requirements as builders look for ways to cut costs.
Renter/Owner Status	Renters may lack access to information about financial resources during recovery. They may not have insurance or (mistakenly) assume that FEMA only assists homeowners and not renters.
Occupation	Jobs that depend on local equipment (manufacturing) or facilities (food industry) may be lost for a long time after a major disaster, leading to long-term unemployment and financial hardship. Conversely, knowledge work, for example, is less tied to location and more resilient.
Family Structure	Single parents with young children are more vulnerable (again, everything is more complicated with little children).
Education	Better education translates into the ability to understand warnings and access recovery information and services. Further, many of our disaster preparedness activities emphasize education and distributing information, which works well for the more educated, but poorly for those less educated.
Medical Services	Health care providers, including physicians, are critical suppliers of relief after an event. Hospitals and nursing homes include more socially vulnerable people.
Social Dependence	People who are fully reliant on social services to survive are already marginalized economically and socially and need additional support in the aftermath of a disaster.
Special Needs	Individuals with disabilities, chronic disease or other characteristics are more dependent on others.

*A few of these examples come from M. Masozera, M. Bailey and C. Kerchner, "Distribution of Impacts of Natural Disasters Across Income Groups: A Case Study of New Orleans," *Ecological Economics* 63 (August 1, 2007): 299-306.

run the risk of actually increasing the gap between those with resources and those without. Third, we argue that by creating a general disaster ministry focusing on the vulnerable (along with specialized preparation) you will be prepared for all forms of disaster.

Understanding Vulnerability

So why are people vulnerable? People can be vulnerable because they are exposed to risk, such as living in an area prone to tornadoes or flooding, but we are interested in a particular kind of vulnerability called social vulnerability.[2] The social vulnerability concept was developed by researchers Susan Cutter, Brian Boruff and Lynn Shirley at the University of South Carolina. It is a way to better understand why some communities suffer greater destruction and have a harder time recovering compared to other communities, even when facing the same type of disaster.

These researchers identified a number of community factors and determined which ones were related to disaster impact and their importance (some factors play a larger role in vulnerability than others). These factors consistently related to the level of destruction and the difficulty in recovery in a community following a disaster. Table 3.1 shows that the factors have a lot to do with resources in the community and access to those resources. Note that the issue is mainly about people—as the people in the community are vulnerable, so is the entire community, including people who may not be directly impacted by the disaster. This list can be used as an assessment guide and help you

consider the needs of people in your church and community whom you may not have thought of as vulnerable.

This list will help you begin to see the importance of community characteristics as well as the characteristics of members of your own church. Research into trauma and recovery is increasingly showing that as people suffer greater levels of trauma and disruption to their lives, their ability to cope and recover has more to do with the nature of the community than with their personal characteristics. Therefore, reducing the ways people are uniquely vulnerable to disasters not only reduces the risk of harm, it also generally improves the ability of the community to help community members cope and recover. This is specifically true for the church. When disaster strikes, people need their church as a source of coping and support, as a resource that strengthens their ability to recover, and as a buffer against the questions about God and faith that inevitably arise. Thus, a prepared church is serving the members and the community that depend upon it.

Justice, Preparedness and Vulnerability

The issue of community and vulnerability goes much deeper than just identifying people at risk. If disaster impact is, as the United Nations says, a combination of the disaster event and vulnerability, then preventing and mitigating disasters must deal with the root causes of vulnerability.[3] Indeed, if we plan and prepare for a disaster, and we fail to consider the particular needs of the vulnerable among us, then we are contributing to the chasm that exists between the less vulnerable and the more vulnerable. This happens simply because the better off among us are better equipped to act on the recommendations for preparedness, compared to the vulnerable. Preparedness does not directly harm the vulnerable, it just moves the better off further ahead while doing proportionately less to help the most vulnerable. It is likely that the majority of preparedness programs and disaster ministries today are susceptible to this charge.

Since vulnerability is fundamentally about such factors as barriers to resources and lack of adequate response to special needs, then it is reasonable to say that vulnerability is basically the result of injustice. People are disadvantaged, some people receive more than others, and some people are treated unfairly (to say the least) because there is injustice in the world. This speaks to an entirely different motivation for engaging in disaster ministry. If disaster ministry is only preparing for some extreme weather, thereby addressing your church's exposure to disaster risk, then it is a necessary sign of good stewardship, but no more.

However, when we see that disaster impact is about both vulnerability and exposure, and when we recognize that by failing to see and respond to this vulnerability we are actually adding to the problem, then disaster ministry speaks to the core values of the church and becomes a basic ministry for the church.[4] We can go further still. When disasters strike, they reveal the vulnerable in the community, which is to say a disaster reveals injustice in the community. The church is God's agent to ad-

dress injustice in the world, and disasters reveal the need for the church to be engaged in the community and correct injustice. Disasters are partly the focus of ministry, as when preparing your church to be safe, and disasters are an indicator of a more basic and at least as important ministry to correct social injustice and reduce vulnerability to harm.

For example, we have been working in Haiti with the Equitas Group, University of Notre Dame Port-au-Prince and Restavek Freedom Foundation to help local churches work with vulnerable children. Since the earthquake, many children have been caught in human trafficking or in a cultural practice called "restavec." Restavec children are often sent by their families to live with a host family in hopes of a better life. However, in many cases they end up as indentured servants and often the victims of abuse. The stresses of the earthquake have resulted in a drastic increase in child abuse. In this case you see one trauma leading to additional trauma. One of the children now getting help from church leaders shared that before this program had begun, he felt "that the world had forgotten us." Thus, churches are now learning how to recognize restavec, provide skilled trauma care and address the needs of the most vulnerable in their communities. This is an example of how the Haitian church is responding to injustices and to the vulnerable.

So what is the church to do? Thomas Pogge, in writing about health care inequality and justice, starts his recommendations by saying first do no harm.[5] What he means by this is to first see where your programs may be adding to injustice. It is surprisingly easy for this to happen unintentionally. Significant gaps exist between the top half of our society and the bottom half in terms of health, access to resources and the impact of disasters. Efforts to close this gap through education and support services have not only been largely ineffective, but also, in some cases, have made the gap larger. Similarly, we have seen where disaster preparedness programs have added to the gap. Those who are better off are usually better educated, are more experienced in putting information into action, and have the resources to support their effort. For example, we held a class on extreme weather safety for refugees in our own community, focusing on people from other countries who had never seen a blizzard or tornado. As soon as we started talking about making "go-kits" we realized our error. How do you ask people who may not have enough food for tomorrow to set aside a week's supply of food? How do they store extra batteries when they already steal batteries out of the fire alarm to use with other devices? We caught our error and started working with the people in the class to come up with solutions. But if we had not caught this, if it was a larger class where the poor might have been overlooked, then it is easy to see who would have gone home and made their kits and who would not. And when the kits were needed, who would be ready and who would not.

Doing "no harm" also applies to the recovery side of the disaster. In the United States, and most countries, recovery starts with rebuilding businesses, especially large employers. We are not suggesting this is a corruption issue—there are sound reasons for this policy—but nevertheless, people who rent, or live in public housing, or have small businesses end up waiting for their recovery assistance. And while they wait, the harm of the disaster continues.

Can the church do anything about policy issues? There are several examples. If a policy makes sense for the community, but the vulnerable will bear a larger share of the burden, then the church can call attention to this and advocate for compensating programs so there is greater justice in community policy. The church can help advocate for people, call attention to the impact on the vulnerable and, by being aware of the problem, use its own ministries to support those in need.

Sometimes corruption is involved. As we said, disaster impact is about both exposure and vulnerability. On top of that, the harm suffered by the vulnerable is multiplied where there is corruption. In Chengdu, during the great Sichuan earthquake, an elementary school collapsed, killing all the schoolchildren who were inside. It was later found that the construction company had somehow been allowed to build the school without using rebar in the walls. The same happened in the poorer areas in Haiti. Haiti has building codes that address earthquake risks, but some contractors were allowed to cut corners, and as a result more buildings collapsed and more people were killed in the poorer areas of Port-au-Prince. While our examples are from the developing world, corruption exists everywhere. Through its ministries, the church is brought closer to those who will bear the burden of corruption and is positioned to speak out on their behalf.

On a more optimistic note, recognizing the essential nature of disaster ministry is a far stronger motivator for the church. When a program or ministry connects to basic values and beliefs, then people become engaged. The ministry goes beyond something that would be nice to do, to something that speaks to who we are as a church. Being prepared so you will have power when the electricity goes out or have a place to meet while the building is repaired is important, but this mindset connects to merely nominal values of stewardship. Being prepared because there are vulnerable people in your church and community who will suffer great and lasting harm calls us to go beyond ourselves and learn who is vulnerable and how to serve them. That is what is meant by a core value that is more engaging and motivating. When a program connects with people at this level, we speak of this as being part of the culture of the church.

From Vulnerability to Resilience

If we need to address the vulnerable, how do we do it? The counter to vulnerability is resilience. Resilience is the ability to bounce back and recover quickly from disaster in a healthy manner.[6] An analogy to resilience is an inflated beach ball in a swimming pool. "When pushed underwater the ball may be stressed (compressed) by the surrounding pressure, but it can resurface quickly near its original shape and position."[7] An effective disaster ministry seeks to build resilience in people, in the church and in the community. Resilience can also be thought of as our ability to do the following:[8]

- bounce back
- take on difficult challenges and still find meaning in life
- respond positively to difficult situations
- rise above adversity
- cope when things look bleak
- tap into hope
- transform unfavorable situations into wisdom, insight and compassion
- endure

Social scientists have observed for many years that some people, churches and communities appear less vulnerable to harm from stress or trauma. Further, when these people do face a crisis or trauma, they appear to recover more quickly. Such people appear to have numerous characteristics that help them to be more resilient, such as access to resources and support, strategies for taking care of themselves, problem-solving skills and an internal dialogue that helps them to see things in a balanced way without becoming overwhelmed.[9] Because of these strengths, a person, church or community may not only be able to cope and recover, but also adapt and become better prepared for the next stressful situation.

Resilience is the most important defense people have against stress. Resilience is important to build and foster readiness for future challenges. You can think of resilience as the development of a reservoir of internal resources to draw upon during stressful situations. As we write elsewhere, "Research has shown that resilience is ordinary, not extraordinary, and that people regularly demonstrate being resilient."[10] Fortunately, resilience is not a trait that people, churches or communities either have or do not have. Rather, it involves behaviors, thoughts and actions that can be learned and developed in anyone. It is also important to remember that resilience is tremendously influenced by a person's environment.

For example, in our trauma work in Africa we learned of the plight of the people of Goma in the eastern Democratic Republic of the Congo. Despite war, genocide and an active volcano, they continue to press forward. Specifically, a community of Christians living in this region fled volcanic ash and lava, then returned to the region, actually making their homes from what had been spewed from Nyiragongo Volcano—this is resilience.

Building Congregational Disaster Resilience

That last point about environment is particularly relevant to the church. Churches can create environments that promote resilience. A resilient church has the ability and capacity to withstand challenges and emergencies by developing the ability to reduce risk, overcome disruptions, adapt and recover. Thus, resilient churches are more likely to be able to resume core ministry operations and functions when faced with adversity.

In fact, many churches already promote resilience-building activities without realizing it or without calling it resilience.

Rather, many churches refer to this process as building community. Examples of ways many churches already foster resilience include promoting small groups, getting people connected and being faithful to those in need.[11] Basically, it is a part of what most churches do as a matter of course. All of these community- and relationship-building efforts also build resilience. These basic things churches can do are very important in disasters when people most need these kinds of resources. We speak further to this point later when we talk about integrating disaster ministry into the basic work of the church.

Being prepared *before* a disaster hits will increase the odds your congregation will be better positioned to help one another but also to help others in the community. But what exactly does the resilient church look like? Obviously, it is not a beach ball bouncing back into shape, but rather a social institution. Thus, the features of resilience in a church are social in nature. A resilient church is one where all sectors of the church community, those with resources and those without, are known to one another and work together to prepare and support one another. The risks they face, and the people most exposed to those risks, are known to the church community. Conversely, churches and communities where groups are isolated and cut off from one another are more vulnerable in the sense that the weak link makes the chain more vulnerable.

In resilient congregations there is a strong sense of being a community that comes from open communication, working together in ministry and creating strong relationships. When a disaster strikes, these relationships and sense of community are a source of support and hope for those who are affected. A resilient congregation is also one that engages other resources that are needed by the community—it is connected to community services and knows what is available, what people can expect in times of need and how to access those resources. For example, churches can build relationships with their local Federal Emergency Management Agency (FEMA), public health, community service and social service offices so that church leaders can serve as a bridge or connector between the church members in need and these resources. Some churches form working relationships with their local agencies for the mutual benefit of helping the agencies better serve the community, and in turn being better able to access resources in times of need. Additionally, a resilient congregation pays attention to infrastructure, asking questions such as the following:

- Who lives in homes vulnerable to hurricane, tornado, flood or heat, and what can be done to reduce their risk?

- Is the climate in the area changing?

- Who is most likely to be affected by those changes?

In resilient churches, the members are continuously working to know who is in need, how well their needs are being met and how to strengthen the weakest or poorest among them. This is a key point to understand. The same vulnerabilities that put people at risk for poverty, disease or other harm also put them at risk in disasters. Therefore, when a church generally addresses those in need within its community it is also reducing disaster risk. Resilient congregations are not just resilient in the face of a natural disaster, but they are also resilient in the face of any threat.

The strategies that lead to a more resilient church can be summarized this way:

- Remove barriers to relationships and cooperation between different members of the church.

- Seek out those who are vulnerable and work as a church to make them less vulnerable.

- Make everyone aware of the risks to themselves and others, and engage them in finding innovative ways to become prepared and maintain their preparedness.

An example of one church that employed these strategies was a church with a large number of elderly members. The congregation became concerned about the risks to these members from a range of threats: flu, flood, heat wave and more. They developed a creative program to teach the adult children of these elderly members how to recognize the risks their parents faced and how to work together to manage those risks, even though many of the children did not live in the community. The church worked with their public health and FEMA offices and had speakers talk with the adult children about the risks and how to manage them. The children helped put together plans, which they did together with their parents, assisted by the church. The church became a bridge between the adult children—whether local or in other communities—

and the elderly members of the church.

If you were to make a list of the characteristics of a resilient congregation, you might see things like this:

- Leadership proactively engaging people in ministry

- Seeking opportunities to change the community for the better (not accepting the status quo)

- Clear communication, not only with those it is easy to communicate with, but with everyone

- Emphasizing learning for all members of the community

- Promoting service to those in need

- Clear responsibilities during crises

- Supportive environment for those in need (avoiding blaming victims for failing to take better care of themselves)

- Sense of being one community

- Close connections among staff, lay leaders and congregation members

- A broad-based volunteerism (everyone looking for a way to play a part)

- Resource sharing across all segments of the community

- Access to services by all

That is what a resilient congregation looks like. Now we will begin to address in the following chapters how to make it happen.

Conclusion

The example of what happened in Forest Heights, Mississippi, after Hurricane Katrina is just one such instance of injustice stemming back generations. As was the case with Hurricane Katrina, disasters not only cause damage, but they also reveal damage in communities that was already there. Disasters do not strike equally across society. Many people are vulnerable in many different ways and in combinations of ways. Those most vulnerable suffer more of the consequences of a disaster and they suffer them for a longer time. Churches are in a special position to help those most vulnerable. This is not just because churches are willing to help, but is also due to the special relationship of trust many churches have with the local community. The church is in a better position to know who is vulnerable and how to reach and serve them. If churches are going to become more resilient, then they need to start by identifying the most vulnerable in their own congregations and communities.

Discussion Questions

1. Who are the vulnerable within your own church? Your community?

2. What are the programs you have for these people, and are the programs informed by what may happen to these people in a disaster?

3. How do your programs make vulnerable people more resilient? If they don't, how might you get started?

Part Two

Planning, Response and Recovery

chapter four

Getting Started

In the fall of 2013, First Presbyterian Church in Glen Ellyn, Illinois, arranged for me (David) to teach an adult education Sunday school class on the topic of church preparedness, disaster relief as a ministry and the biblical call to serve neighbors, community and the world.[1] Many members of our First Presbyterian small group attended the Sunday school classes. As a result of this class, our small group decided to take on the project of engaging our church in disaster ministry, including laying out a framework for crisis management at our church. We began by finding out what had already been done by other groups. This involved collecting information from a variety of sources, including some group members attending workshops on disasters and crisis management in houses of worship. Other members gathered information on the Internet, held informal meetings with the church staff and met with members of the community who work in the area of crisis relief.

The group wanted to use our small group resources in ways that would be most beneficial to the church, not re-create

something that other churches had already done. We were pleasantly surprised to find a wealth of information, templates, planning strategies and so on in books, magazine articles, community groups and online. Many churches and community organizations generously shared what they learned in developing their own strategic plans. Some offered templates that could be freely customized and used.

A group member approached the church session for approval to develop a plan. After approval, the pastor, church staff and session offered to help in whatever way they could. We then decided we needed more basic information about what had been done in the past regarding disaster planning and what still existed. At our next group meeting we discussed taking the following actions:

1. Create a risk assessment survey to see what group members thought were the major risks to our church.

2. Conduct a facilities audit of the church property.

3. Identify "first responders" currently within the church congregation—

medically trained people (doctors, nurses, pharmacists, special medical certifications) and law enforcement (police, FBI agents, firefighters, EMS trained).

4. Determine what is already being done by the church or other church members, such as existing preschool risk plans, usher training and any other planning or training.

5. Meet with the property committee to find out about exit plans, building security, keys and so on.

6. Inventory emergency medical resources (defibrillator, first-aid supplies, etc.).

7. Make a list of available resources.

At our next small group meeting, we started feeling the weight of the task we had created for ourselves and decided that we had been too ambitious in the scope of our plan. We needed to start small and develop a single plan on a specific issue relating to a crisis-management program. At the end of the project, we would then turn the plan and a proposal for ministry over to the church staff and the session. Having a specific focus helped the group to not feel overwhelmed and potentially lose interest, which was a risk if we covered too many areas at the onset of the project. There was also some concern about our small group becoming the disaster group, which was not our intent. We wanted to be the spark plug, not the entire engine. Having a specific focus would allow us to launch the project, and then allow a separate group to continue the work while our small group went back to being a small group.

We used our risk assessment to help us select the starting place. We asked ourselves to prioritize possible crisis situations to determine which we thought were most urgent to address. We also sought to determine what our members had a special interest in doing. We chose as our project the situation of a hostile intruder/shooter entering the church. Here are some of the steps we took as a result of this decision: We started by viewing a short video titled "Run, Hide, Fight," which depicts survival strategies in a hostile intruder/shooter situation. We then invited a member of the church's properties committee to attend one of our group meetings. She answered questions about the church's building and facilities pertaining to safety, exits and so on. We discussed how the committee could work with the small group's plan. Next we met with the church staff about our plans. After that we contacted the Glen Ellyn Police Department Community Liaison, who did a walk-through and safety assessment of the church grounds.

We received feedback from some staff and church members that they didn't want to scare people away from church by focusing only on a violent intruder as our initial foray into a safety project. This was useful feedback, especially considering that there hadn't ever been any incidents of this type in the church's history. As a result of this input, we modified our plan to a more generalized term of a disruptive person in church. This more inclusive term covered situations that had occurred in our church, such as an intoxicated person entering the church or someone wanting to confront a pastor, and it included active shooters. The hope was that the congregation and staff would more easily see a need for a plan such as this and be supportive of changes that might be implemented.

As we worked our way through the changes and modifications of our plan, it became apparent in our group that we wanted to launch something that a few of us would continue to work with while also engaging the church leadership and other interested members. We decided the small group would "give birth" to both a specific plan for managing disruptions and a general description of how to move forward to develop a larger program. We would then propose that a new group be formed from some within the group who had a greater interest in putting together a plan, and interested leaders in the church. This new group would facilitate the continuing development of this ministry, both by helping existing ministries to be more "disaster aware" and also creating specific plans for managing extreme events.

Our final plan came together in two parts: a plan for managing disruptive intruders, including resources and links to training, and a framework for the larger ministry showing how this plan fit into an overall approach to ministry. We hoped this overall view would serve as a blueprint for the disaster ministry committee. Putting this together included three helpful things:

- Watching several online videos for usher training pertaining to dealing with a disruptive congregant and assessing a person's behavior prior to their entering the sanctuary to determine if they could potentially become disruptive.

- Discussing that this type of project needs to have a champion(s)—someone who will help others stay motivated in their commitment to a safety plan in the church.

- Talking about how this type of project would need continued participation by the more interested members of our group if we hoped to continue its viability. This led to a discussion about whether the project could be handed off to the session or if a separate group dealing solely with safety issues needed to be formed within the church.

We learned a few things that might be of help to you. First, start small. Be very concrete about what you hope to accomplish and establish a timeline to completion. This will help your group feel successful and be able to reflect on a completed project. Second, your project will change as you learn more on this topic and the specific needs of your church. Be open to this continuing refinement of your project. You will ultimately end up with a better plan than what you started with. Third, don't re-create the wheel. There are many resources out there, and most are free of charge. Use them as a starting point, then customize them to suit the needs of your church. Fourth, members of your group will have different levels of interest in this type of project. Keeping the project time limited helps keep people motivated. Finally, it is not all about creating new ministries. Help people to see how their current ministry can be strengthened by being disaster aware.[2]

Purpose

While most congregation leaders agree disaster ministry is important, that is different from understanding what to do. In our conversations with congregation leaders, the biggest challenge they expressed was simply getting started in this ministry. In this chapter, we present the various ways different congregations have approached disaster ministry, the types of programs they started and how they began. There is no one approach that fits everyone. Hopefully, in the pages that follow, you will see an approach that works for your congregation.

Build on Prayer and the Congregation's Theological Tradition

Whenever I (Jamie) consult with church leaders who are interested in starting a disaster ministry, I always begin by encouraging churches to spend time reflecting in prayer about how God might use them in the event of a disaster. I also encourage them to pray for guidance about the vulnerable in their congregations and communities. This is a time for them to pray about how God would have them utilize their church's unique resources and ministries to help those in need. It is common for me to also ask the leaders I am working with to consider their theology of disasters. In most cases I get asked, "What do you mean disaster theology?" What I have found is that most of us do not have a very sophisticated framework for understanding the theological implications of disasters. Maybe we have never even really thought about it explicitly. But after some prompting I have found that in all actuality

we have at least an implicit reference for making meaning and sense of disasters. For example, thousands of sermons and Bible studies are held all over the world on topics like pain and suffering and the sovereignty of God. Therein lies our theology of disaster, and that is where your church should start getting ready for a disaster.

The way you prepare, plan and respond to disasters should be built on your theology. For example, after Hurricane Katrina there was a large Southern Baptist church along the coast that started a chainsaw ministry. Here was a church whose theology suggested that God had provided each of them with a gift that could be used to help those affected by this horrendous storm. It just so happened that in this case, many of the men in the congregation worked as chainsaw operators among the vast pine forest farms. They played an important role in the recovery process by removing trees from out of people's homes, yards and roads, and in doing so sharing the gospel and witness of Christ. Then there was an Episcopal church whose theology was very social-justice oriented who noticed that many homeowners who struggled to make mortgage payments every month before the storm could not get back into their homes after the storm. You see, even if people had insurance, the cost to rebuild their homes had gone up beyond what most were insured for because of the increased cost in materials and insurance premiums. Thus, this church decided to make small microloans to help these struggling families by filling the gap between their insurance coverage and costs caused by inflation.

Know Your Strengths

Each congregation has its own unique resources (some more than others) that could be leveraged for a disaster ministry. Be sure to assess both your physical resources, such as space or food preparation, and the resources represented by the individuals within your congregation. For example, networks of relationships are strengths: connections with government, knowledge of service programs and how to access them, and the ability to advocate for those who need help accessing resources. Determining the skills and resources within your congregation will allow you to determine what type of disaster ministry is possible for your particular church.

Be Aware of Challenges of Getting Started

Despite having the desire and motivation to start a disaster ministry, there are often barriers that prevent getting started. Given the risk and the potential to serve those in need, why aren't more churches prepared to help their members and their community? Common barriers include a lack of staff, funds, volunteers, time or other resources. Other common obstacles for creating a disaster ministry are a lack of information on how to plan, organize and start. There are several possible explanations.

One common barrier is the challenge of preparing for the infrequent and unpredictable event. Churches and other organizations in areas where disasters strike with regularity are prepared. They see the cost of being unprepared, and they know it is probable they will pay that cost if they do

not act. This does not, however, apply to most churches. Most churches, like the people that attend and belong to them, are busy with many programs that address the real, immediate needs of their members and community. From this perspective, disaster preparedness is a lot of effort for something that may never be needed when there are already more needs than resources. This view is a cost benefit analysis, and disaster preparedness is a cost that might not yield a benefit.

A second explanation is related to the first: too narrow a view of disaster and disaster ministry. This explanation points out that too often people think that a disaster ministry means cleaning up after a hurricane or tornado, or rescuing people during a flood (i.e., that it is a crisis response ministry). As such, it is an add-on that is implemented when the crisis strikes, but not a part of the ongoing work of the church. Thus, disaster ministry becomes a focus for a few people, but not well integrated into the church, and not seen as part of the real work of the church.

A third barrier is that people fail to recognize the very real threats around them, and thus do not take steps to be prepared. This is due in large part to our fascination with the extreme events that leave the impression that the only disasters are the extreme weather disasters, or possibly the terrorist threat. People may be unaware of the chemical plant at the edge of town that could leak dangerous fumes, the train that goes through the middle of town carrying toxic chemicals or that heat wave that will kill the residents of the local nursing home once the power (and the AC) goes out.[3]

Engage Leadership

We have found Convoy of Hope's four-step approach to engaging church leadership in disaster ministry to be a useful example for getting others involved.[4] A successful disaster ministry begins (and ends) with leadership. This involves getting key congregational leadership on board with your vision for a disaster ministry. It also encompasses identifying and developing the right leaders to help you carry out your disaster ministry. The way leadership looks and evolves can vary greatly from church to church, as highlighted by the story at the start of this chapter. For some churches, the idea of starting and building a disaster ministry begins with senior church leadership. However, we have found that in many cases, the average senior church leader is already overwhelmed with a wide range of responsibilities. It can be hard for senior leadership to take on yet another role and ministry. Thus, we have found it is often a lay leader with a heart for serving others in times of crisis that gets a disaster ministry started. Following are some tips for engaging others in forming a disaster ministry.

Get the senior leadership of the church on board with starting a disaster ministry. While I was living in Mississippi I received a grant to help minority churches start a disaster ministry. Over the course of a year I worked closely with about twenty African American and Vietnamese churches. Each of the churches that took part in the project appointed a lay leader to serve as their disaster ministry coordinator (see below for more details). At the end of the year, each church reported on what had helped them the most in terms of getting started. Each of the disaster ministry coordinators said that it was having the support of their senior church leaders. They said it made all the difference having their pastor endorse the program and commission their ministry. Overall, having senior leadership on board is essential to establishing the credibility of your disaster ministry.

Identify a disaster ministry coordinator. You've heard it said that "too many cooks in the kitchen" can be a challenge. The same is true when planning a disaster ministry. It's typically best to have one primary point person to head up the group. (However, as a quick aside, you want to make sure there are one or more persons who could step in after a disaster in case this person is not available because of their own disaster experience.) The African American and Vietnamese churches we mentioned frequently referred to those in this position as their disaster ministry coordinator, though, if you look around at some of the various manuals out there on the topic, you'll see there's no "one" term. Use whatever fits your congregation best.

Overall, the disaster ministry coordinator should be someone your church can count on: a self-starter, a person others respect. It would also be helpful if this person has some previous experience that might help them in this role. Perhaps you have someone in your church who currently serves on the local fire department or in an emergency management related field. If not, no worries. Look for someone who has strong leadership skills. It's also a good idea to look for someone whose overall giftings and passion are related to serving others in times of crisis. The disaster ministry coordinator should be approved and empowered by senior church leadership.

Establish a disaster ministry team. Once you select a disaster ministry coordinator, it is time to identify a *disaster ministry team* to coordinate the development activities. There are several reasons for taking a team approach. One, the responsibility for starting and especially implementing a disaster ministry is often more than one person can realistically take on. Two, if a disaster hits your community, there is a chance that some of those serving on the team will be directly affected. Having a team increases your odds that at least some members on the team are not directly affected (or at least not affected as badly as others) and are still available to carry out their ministry duties.[5] When selecting team members, it can be helpful to keep the following in mind.

All pertinent areas of the local church should be represented by individuals who have knowledge of each ministry and/or operations process. For example, a typical congregation might have ministry representation from nursery, children, youth, music and ushers, plus business operations like accounting, payroll, IT, facilities and security. Representation will vary depending on church composition, as well as critical ministries and operation functions. You may also find it useful to include church members who work in law enforcement, public utilities, health care and the military. The quality of leaders recruited for a leadership team directly correlates to the quality of your congregation's ability to successfully prepare. We recommend recruiting leaders who have

strong leadership skills and influence. Strong leadership skills are necessary to make sure all delegated tasks are completed on schedule and meet agreed-upon expectations. Leaders with influence in business and/or the congregation or the emergency management and first responder system have access to other leaders and resources that can greatly add to your congregation's resilience.

Although a large group may want to participate in disaster preparedness and response planning, larger groups tend to lose focus. Keep the initial disaster ministry team to approximately six to ten individuals. Once goals are established, include more members of the congregation as necessary. If your congregation is small, you may have the disaster ministry team doing all of the work of the ministry. In a larger church, or in a regional network, the ministry team is more of a coordinating team that supports several specific action teams, such as one focusing on planning, another on emergency response and perhaps one on training. Again, this will likely vary from church to church depending on your size and scope of ministries.[6]

Select a Disaster Ministry Model That Best Fits Your Congregation

Each congregation is unique in its values, culture, resources available and in various other ways. As we have stated, the way to create and start a disaster ministry for your congregation will look different from other congregations. There are countless ways that you could shape and form a disaster ministry. To help you get started we discuss three overarching or "umbrella" models that capture most of these approaches. The point of these models is to help churches see the range of possibilities and to especially see how different disaster ministries can advance the core mission of the church as a window to the kingdom of God. They are not exclusive models; it is feasible that a church may follow one or a combination of these approaches.

The first approach we will describe, the *disaster-informed ministry model*, encourages churches to think about building resilience strategies into their ongoing ministries. Rather than establishing a whole new ministry, you work to prepare your already established ministries to be ready to adapt to disaster circumstances. This is also referred to as making your existing ministries "disaster aware" (one of the strategies in this chapter's case study), where participants ask themselves questions like, What will become of the people we serve if a disaster strikes? What disasters are those we serve most vulnerable to? And, How can we embed assessment of risk and preparedness into our current ministry? The second main approach we will discuss can be thought of as a *specialized disaster ministry*, where a church actually launches a new ministry that focuses almost exclusively on disasters. In most cases these types of disaster ministries have a strong emergency response component aimed at meeting unmet needs in the wake of catastrophe (e.g., providing meals to disaster survivors). As you read the examples below, consider your congregation's strengths, the needs of your local community and the resources and motivation of your members when determining

an approach that best fits your place and people. A third approach we will discuss is the *disaster ministry network model*. In this case, churches collaborate with each other or with other faith-based organizations to develop a broader community response to disasters.

The disaster-informed ministry model. One way to approach disaster ministry is to integrate it into your other programs or ministries rather than create a new ministry. To approach this, you ask how the people served in your existing ministries are vulnerable when disaster strikes. As a first step, you might assess the ministries that already exist in your congregation to see where disaster ministry can be incorporated. The advantage of this approach is that it avoids narrowly focusing the disaster ministry on responding to natural disasters. There is nothing wrong with that focus except that it may unnecessarily exclude people whose priorities are with other ministries. Start with an existing ministry and ask how this ministry and the people it serves are vulnerable to disaster. If the ministry is a church school, does the school have a disaster plan? Does the school educate parents to have home disaster plans? You do not need a disaster ministry to do this; you just need to be aware that disasters cut across all other programs because they impact everything and everyone. Integrating disaster ministry keeps the disaster focus contained to the existing programs and helps people to think through the full scope of risks. Or if you have a visitation ministry, the people involved in this ministry can be provided with a disaster risk checklist and given an orientation to the kinds of risks faced by the people they visit. They can then observe how people are at risk and either assist them in being better prepared or alert the church that there are people who will definitely need help if disaster strikes.

Further, a disaster-informed approach emphasizes prevention and preparedness and avoids defining disaster ministry as a crisis-driven episodic program. Other examples of disaster-informed ministries include services to the elderly, such as transportation or Meals on Wheels. Afterschool tutoring provides a way to see who are the poor and vulnerable families, such as migrant workers or immigrants, who may not be familiar with disaster risks and what to do about them. A support program for single parents or young mothers is another example of a ministry that is a window into the lives of vulnerable people (a single parent with young children is at very high risk in a disaster). All these programs allow you to see who is vulnerable to the types of disasters that are likely in your area without creating a specific disaster ministry.

This disaster-informed approach can be an easy place to start. It does not require a new program or large investment of resources, and it generally can be implemented quickly. It is easier to maintain preparedness when it is part of another program rather than a separate program, and it encourages you to build on your strengths. For example, if you have a strong children's ministry, start there. This would allow you to build on what you do well and "pivot" your programming, resources and focus onto emergencies that arise in your congregation and community.

There may be an even more basic and compelling reason to consider a disaster-informed approach to this ministry. We suggested earlier that disasters are a test of ministry and community. Considering the disaster-related needs of those you already serve can reveal how well you know the ways and extent that the people you serve are vulnerable. A disaster-informed ministry becomes a more broadly effective ministry, going beyond the specific focus of the ministry to also address less apparent but very significant needs. Put another way, it helps your program shift from focusing on the specific provision of a service to a better understanding of the people, especially vulnerable people, who are the focus of that program.

Specialized disaster ministry model. A second common approach many churches use to develop a disaster ministry is to follow a specialized disaster ministry model. The emphasis is on emergency response and needs. In these cases, churches create an entirely new ministry that is specific to disasters that are likely in their area. Some churches may also develop specialized disaster ministries that are equipped and ready to deploy to other communities affected by disasters. The specialized ministry is what most people think of when they think "disaster response." A few examples of a specialized disaster ministry model include churches with staff and/or volunteers ready to clean up after a tornado, create chainsaw gangs and run food trucks. Churches operating specialized disaster ministries may also have shelter, evacuation and rescue team plans in place.

We recently completed a project looking at the different ways congregations prepared for disasters in Cook County and Chicago. Several of the churches that developed a specialized disaster ministry had active Community Emergency Response Teams (CERT).[7] The CERT program is offered through FEMA and other local emergency management agencies to train teams in basic disaster response skills, such as fire safety, light search and rescue, team organization and disaster medical operations. Thus, many of the churches taking this approach to disaster ministry had a group of highly skilled volunteers that were prepared and ready to deploy in response to local emergencies.

For example, St. Paul's Lutheran Church has provided CERT training since 2007. Their CERT team is ready to provide the following services: simple rescue, simple triage, transport of victims, basic firefighting skills, sandbagging skills and helping members handle or turn off home utilities. The idea of forming a CERT team started when some members of St. Paul's assisted in tornado and hurricane recovery. Although they got the job done, the members noticed problems with the disorganized system and decided to begin a CERT team to be better prepared should a disaster strike their own community. Examples of activities they have been involved with include preparing sandbags for potential floods and assisting a local hospital during a large medical emergency.

A congregation that chooses this approach will need to take stock and make sure they have the internal resources among members to support this ministry.

These resources may include skilled volunteers, funding, equipment, time and infrastructure (i.e., capacity). We have seen examples of churches that lacked in one or more of these areas and as a result found themselves encountering numerous struggles. For example, a study of church responses following Superstorm Sandy in New York found a few churches actually had to close their doors because they overextended themselves financially.[8] Similarly, there was a church on the West Coast that had a "shelter in place" (which involves staying at the church during the peak of a disaster) to help with emergencies but did not screen volunteers from their church. Sadly, one of the volunteers had a criminal record as a pedophile and molested a child at the shelter. The church was sued and almost lost their building in the suit. We do not share these examples to discourage adopting this sort of model. Rather, we share these examples so that you can take some simple steps to help avoid these types of challenges.

At the same time, we have seen examples of churches with few resources that have been able to develop quite successful specialized disaster ministries. After Hurricane Katrina I studied how smaller churches were responding. I did an interview with a pastor of a small church that was hit hard from the storm in Biloxi, Mississippi. This was a small church, maybe twenty or so members, most of whom were living below or just above the poverty line. The pastor was also bi-vocational, meaning that he spent about one day a week at the church while holding down another full-time job. During the interview he pulled out a small newspaper article that detailed how his church had formed a specialized disaster ministry around one widow in their congregation. She had lost everything and had no family in the area. They helped her rebuild her home, brought her meals, made sure she was taking her medicine, and visited and prayed with her. In this case they provided some very specialized assistance, but did so on a scale that was reasonable for a church of their size and with the resources they had.

Overall, if your plan is to create a specialized disaster ministry, the best thing you can do to get started (and to avoid some of the pitfalls we have highlighted) is to contact local officials involved in doing disaster work. In our experience, we found law enforcement, emergency management, fire departments and public health departments to be extremely helpful. In fact, most churches do not realize that many of these local civil organizations actually have staff who serve as liaisons to the community, which includes working with churches. For example, the Federal Emergency Management Agency (FEMA) employs voluntary agency liaisons who work with nonprofit groups, including churches and faith-based organizations, to help support their disaster relief efforts.[9] Other great resources for starting a specialized disaster ministry include established nongovernmental organizations (NGOs). Two groups found in most regions include state chapters of Voluntary Organizations Active in Disaster (VOAD)[10] and local chapters of the American Red Cross.[11] By consulting with these groups, you will find trained volunteers and/or professionals with years

of rich experience that can help provide your church with additional training, support and resources. They can also help you understand local rules and regulations and possibly liability issues that you need to take into account.

Oakdale Covenant Church in Chicago, Illinois, held an emergency preparedness training for local congregations. The Cook County Public Health Department and American Red Cross facilitated the workshop, while the church provided the space and helped recruit other congregations to attend. Around thirty people attended. They are now taking the next step in holding a brainstorming meeting on how to take the information that they learned and put it into action within their church and their community. This is just one of the many ways congregations might reach out to local authorities and resources for help getting started.

Disaster ministry network model. A third common approach or model is to join with other congregations or faith-based disaster organizations in your area to create a network or new disaster ministry together. This approach allows each member of the network to focus on a part of the overall program that best fits with their members. It also reduces the administrative burden and allows some resources to be shared more efficiently. Again, this can take on many different shapes and sizes, so to speak. In some cases it may mean that you agree to work with another church in your community. Or perhaps you decide to work with a large Christian relief organization to host their volunteer teams in the event of a disaster. It could also mean joining an established ministerial association or network in your community, state or region that focuses on disasters.

While on a project trip to Japan after the tsunami and earthquake, a pastor shared with our team, "One of our biggest sins was not working together or with the community before the disaster struck." In this statement, the pastor was highlighting the importance of working together before a disaster strikes so that there are bonds and relationships in place when you need them the most. All too often churches try and go about disaster preparedness (and response) alone. Most disaster needs are larger than one church can handle alone. Also reflected in the statement from the Japanese pastor was the notion that the churches waited until after the disaster before starting to collaborate. This is not a problem just in Japan. After Hurricane Sandy we received a call from a town commissioner on the coast of New Jersey. He shared the story of how a food truck, equipped by a local church with more than enough food for the area, pulled in to feed the local people and relief workers. Within fifteen minutes a second equally large truck pulled in behind it, and then a third. The commissioner called us to ask if we knew how to get these churches to communicate and coordinate their efforts so there would not be so much waste. Thus, we encourage you that if you are thinking about taking a disaster ministry networking model, try to get it started and running before a disaster strikes rather than waiting until after something bad has occurred. This will save you a lot of headaches.

Here's another example of what a di-

saster ministry network model might look like. Along the Mississippi coast there is a disaster ministry task force that was started after Hurricane Camille (1969). It would reactivate after a major disaster hit the coast and then go dormant again after the recovery process was complete. However, Hurricane Katrina changed the way this group of local churches worked together. They realized that trying to establish new relationships and trying to respond together after a disaster was really too late. Therefore the task force did not shut down and is still running. I had the opportunity to collaborate with this network during my time in Mississippi. Because they continued to meet and work together regularly, this group was able to respond not just to Katrina, but to other disasters, including Hurricane Gustav, the H1N1 outbreak and the Deepwater Horizon oil spill. To stay active, they have also focused on other community needs that may not fit the definition of a disaster but have definitely affected people, such as the economic recession and health disparities. This helped keep relationships and skills sharp in between disasters.

As demonstrated in the aforementioned example, effective networks are built on relationships, and ultimately response largely depends on preexisting relationships. Thus, we would encourage churches to consider how they might leverage their gifts and strengths by partnering with other churches and organizations. In doing so, churches are poised to operate as the full body of Christ—with each church bringing their resources to the table. This not only creates important ties, but also has a multiplying effect on our ability to respond.

Another way that churches might partner together is to consider developing "sister" church relationships. That is, your church might come to an agreement with other churches that you will help each other in the event of a disaster. Again, you do not want to go through a disaster alone. Recovery takes place in community. If the disaster is large enough, you and your sister church may both be affected. Therefore, you will also want to partner with another church outside your region.

My local church in Mississippi partnered with a church in Indiana when Hurricane Gustav threatened. The church in Indiana agreed to watch the storm and send help if my church was affected. They also agreed to staff people around the clock on the church phones so that members from my church could call in (once they got a phone signal) to let others know they were okay and to share needs, creating a check-in point of sorts. Fortunately my church went unscathed, but it was reassuring to our congregation to know there were other churches ready to come to our aid if we needed them.

Conclusion

The examples provided in this chapter are just some options that could help you launch your disaster ministry. Leaders and congregation members can be creative in their starting process. Certain congregations may customize the options that were listed, while others may find that a completely different option works better for them. When determining the right type of disaster ministry for your church, keep in mind the values and goals of your congregation as well as the type of populations that your congregation typically serves. Additionally, it may be better for some congregations to start by serving the members of their own congregation before creating a larger ministry to serve their community. Now that you have a framework for a disaster ministry, in the next chapter we discuss how to start planning for it.

Discussion Questions

1. How does (or would) a disaster ministry fit with the basic aims of your church?

2. How would you as a leader communicate this alignment with the aims of the church so that the entire membership understands this ministry as part of the core ministries of the church?

3. How will leadership demonstrate ongoing support for this ministry?

chapter five

Planning

In 2008 Hurricane Gustav threatened the Gulf Coast. On the Friday before the storm was projected to make landfall in Mississippi I (Jamie) got a phone call as I was about to head to lunch. The person on the other line asked, "Are you the disaster guy?" I was caught a little off-guard and, not knowing who exactly he was looking for, asked for some clarification. He went on to inquire if I was the university researcher in the area who had been working with churches since Katrina had hit. To that description I said, "Yes."

He quickly shared with me that he was a minister at a new church, not even a year old. He went on to explain that he was calling because the church leadership was meeting over lunch to try and get a disaster preparedness plan together before the storm hit. I changed my lunch plans and headed for the meeting. When I arrived I found a group of five church leaders. They informed me that the church was so new that they did not have a full congregation emergency contact list, let alone a disaster plan in place. They went on to describe their congregation members as being largely young couples and families living in a historic and diverse neighborhood.

As I mentioned in the last chapter, I began by encouraging them to prayerfully approach the process and to consider how their theology might guide their plans. From there I began offering some examples of how they might get started, but with every example I shared, they shot down my ideas. "That just won't work for us," I kept hearing. So I sat back in my chair and listened for a few minutes. I realized that the reason many of my ideas were not working was because I was asking these church leaders to try and invent something new rather than work with what already worked well for them.

After a few minutes I interjected with a question: "Do you have church potluck dinners?" I received some pretty surprised looks and reactions from those sitting around the table. I'm sure my question felt very out of place with what we were talking about. Then one of the church leaders said, "Do we have church potluck dinners? We have some of the best church potluck dinners you've ever been to." I went on to ask how they communicated about and organized these gatherings. I found out that this congregation was pretty tech savvy and used Google Docs (an online document sharing tool). They'd ask people to share if they were coming and to sign up to bring specific foods or drinks, as well as to let them know if they had any special dietary restrictions or allergies that the leadership should be aware of.

I asked them what they thought about using this same approach to preparing for Hurricane Gustav. They were on board. Thus, rather than asking if people were coming to a church dinner, we asked them to share their contact and emergency contact information. We asked if they planned on evacuating, and how to best get in touch with them if the storm hit. We also changed questions on the form they normally used in order to inquire if people felt safe where they were planning on riding out the storm or if they needed safer housing options. Rather than food allergies, the leadership asked about possible medical needs people might have if the community was struck by Gustav. Instead of what food or drink people were going to bring to a meal, they were asked if they had supplies that could be used to assist with recovery, and so on.

The church leaders were able to develop this simple yet very sophisticated approach to planning by the time our shared meal was over. They then emailed the survey shortly after along with some updates from the local emergency management agency about the approaching disaster. They also encouraged members to leverage their small groups by agreeing to look out for each other and to check in on one another should the disaster hit. Based on the Google Docs survey responses, the leaders got in touch with members who said they didn't feel safe and paired them up with others who had agreed to allow people to stay with them or had other resources available. Finally, they asked their membership to come to church to discuss how to get ready on the eve of the storm if they were not evacuating. During this time they helped people in their church who weren't as tech savvy or didn't have Internet to complete the survey. They also addressed other needs they hadn't thought about that arose from people taking the survey and discussed their plan at length over the course of the service.[1]

Purpose

This chapter will help you identify areas of concern and establish a plan for your congregation and your family, which will lay the foundation for successful preparedness. Disaster ministry plans need to address a range of events and emergencies caused both by nature and by people, including all-hazards and public health emergencies. As a result, planning may seem overwhelming. However, we want to reassure you that though it takes time and effort, it is manageable. In this chapter we will help you learn how to accomplish the following:

1. Conduct a disaster risk assessment for your congregation and community

2. Engage leadership in developing a disaster ministry vision and goals

3. Develop a continuity of ministry and operations plan (COMOP)

4. Test and practice your plan

Step 1: Conduct a Disaster Risk Assessment for Your Congregation and Community

Assessing risk is an important task that must occur routinely to prepare for emergencies and help reduce the impact of disasters. A good place to start a risk assessment is by discussing and describing past disasters and emergencies affecting your congregation and community. Being aware of past disasters and emergencies can help you identify future threats to include in your plan. We recommend that your team create a list of disasters and emergencies, including public health emergencies, that occurred over the last twenty-five to fifty years in your community. It is also a good idea to reach out to your local emergency management and public health agencies to find out more about likely risks. This could be done simply by sending an email or making a brief call. You might even consider asking a representative from their agency to join one of your meetings.

Looking back is a good strategy for assessing risk, but looking forward into what might be is just as important. Changes in climate, severe weather patterns, population shifts, national security threats, etc., mean we can't just rely on what has happened before in our community. To truly help our congregations assess risk means that we need to also imagine worst-case scenarios that may not have happened before.

For example, in the years that followed 9/11, I (Jamie) was asked to collaborate with an organization that helps the government think about issues related to community and national resilience. A few of the organization's team members had reached out to me to help them consider what terrorist attacks might look like if carried out in small-town USA. I won't go into detail for obvious reasons, but we were able to identify a series of potential threats unique to rural America that are not as likely in urban America. To help your congregation think about what could happen, you might consider the following questions:

1. With all the changes happening in the world, how might the threats to our community change in the future?

2. How do we think our community might change in the near future? And would these changes put us at greater risk?

3. What are our community's strongest resources?

4. Even though there are benefits to the resources we've identified, could there be risks that go hand in hand with those benefits that we've not considered?

Our tendency is to focus on the negative in our community when we think of risk. But our assets can also put us at risk. The discovery of oil has been good in many ways for the state of North Dakota, but at the same time, the increase in industry has raised risk for environmental hazards and technical disasters.[2] Now that you have given attention to what has and could happen, it is time to weigh the likelihood of these happening in your community.

Determine risks. Once your list of potential threats has been created, the next step is to rank them from most likely to least likely to occur. A couple years after Hurricane Katrina I drove about four hours north of the coast to the Mississippi Delta region to meet with a pastoral association to talk about church disaster preparedness. Shortly after I began the meeting, one of the pastors said, "There's never been a hurricane ever reach all the way up here, so I honestly don't know why we all need to be here." His statement caught me off-guard, and I was trying to collect my thoughts when I had to pause the meeting because a train passing along the tracks behind the church was drowning our voices out. I then asked the pastors where the train was going and what the train was likely carrying. One of them explained that it ran from a local refinery to a plant, carrying oil and different chemicals. At about that time, the pastor who had questioned the meeting said, "How about you continue with this talk you came to give." Though their churches were not at risk of a hurricane, they did face some very real threats. This example shows you that no matter where your church is located, there are risks.

After looking at your list you may feel a bit overwhelmed. It is helpful to keep in mind that there is no way any one church can possibly prepare for every type and form of disaster. Keep in mind, where the probability of a disaster and severity of consequence overlap, that is where you should focus your attention. Said differently, you want to prepare for the worst-case scenarios.[3] If you can prepare for those, then your church will likely be prepared to respond to smaller threats by default. It's similar to the sermon illustration where the rocks are placed into a glass jar and then filled up with sand versus filling up the jar with the sand and then the rocks. Taking care of the big stuff makes taking care of the little stuff easier.

Identify vulnerable members of your congregation. Building on the thoughts we shared earlier about the role of the church in responding to injustices, we encourage you to identify vulnerable members of your congregation. You might start by generating a list of members with special needs, identifying them through observations, known relationships, or by handing out a questionnaire (e.g., before or after a worship service) and/or emailing a questionnaire to congregation members. Look for reoccurring special needs as well as geographic concentrations of at-risk congregation members. Examples of at-risk members include (you can expand this list using the social vulnerability section discussed earlier):

- elderly
- people with serious or chronic medical conditions
- differently abled persons
- single parents with small children
- immigrants and refugees
- children

Once you have identified the vulnerable in your own congregation, we would challenge you to repeat this process, but this time, focus on the vulnerable in your community.[4]

Know the congregation's facilities and building. In the same way you have discussed risks to people in your congregation and community, you should also discuss risks related to your church's assets. Assess potential property hazards that might occur if a disaster struck. One way to do this is to have your disaster ministry team walk through the church building and property in search of potential risks. Places you might want to pay particularly close attention to include nurseries, utility rooms, playgrounds, outside structures and storage areas. You can think of this as a safety audit of sorts. Potential risks uncovered should be documented. Further, steps should be taken to perform regular maintenance and should be checked regularly. A church I used to attend has a staff person in charge of facilities management. He shared that he has developed relationships with a small group of other colleagues and volunteers in similar roles at their respective churches. They get together once a month, rotating churches, and actually do a walk-through together of each other's churches. He said that having outside individuals do this task helps to bring new "eyes" and new insights.

As part of this process, it can be helpful to create site maps that include information about the congregation's sanctuary, offices, meeting rooms, hallways, stairwells, location of utility shutoffs and potential staging sites. Consider sharing these maps with local emergency responders ahead of time so that they could be used should a disaster occur. They can also help inform church attendees about where to go in the event of an emergency. This will help leadership identify congregants in need of care, take a head count to ensure no one is remaining inside and aid families in rejoining their children.

Step 2: Engage Leadership in Developing a Disaster Ministry Vision and Goals

Now that you know the possible risks and hazards that your church and community might face in the future, it is time to create a disaster ministry vision and goals. You want your disaster ministry vision and goals to align with the overall vision and goals of your church. We have observed that when a disaster ministry begins to stray from their church's guiding mission, problems start to happen. Maybe part of your church's vision and goals is to minister to those living in poverty in your community. Then that's the place your disaster ministry vision and goals should begin. For some disaster ministry teams the vision and goals may appear almost identical except for the addition of the word *disasters* at the end of their statement. Others may be rooted in their church's mission but can explore unique ways this mission might grow and branch out in the wake of disaster.

The next step is to ask what type of ministry goals you may have and where to start. Consider the following questions drawn from HDI's *Ready Faith: Planning Guide:*[5]

- *Are you new to this type of work?* Starting small and learning is the best practice. Develop a program focusing on your own members and learn from that before launching a large program.

- *Do you have ministries that can be incorporated into a disaster ministry?* Ministries to special populations, like young families, the elderly, the medically infirm and so on, can easily be integrated into a disaster ministry. Do you have a food ministry (like Meals on Wheels), an outreach to immigrants or refugees, or an education ministry? These ministries can be ideal places to start when developing a disaster ministry.

- *Do you have people in your church with expertise in this area?* Among your members, are there employees of FEMA? Local, state or county public health agencies? Or people who work for relief organizations? These people represent an ideal asset for your program, and you should make every effort to recruit them to your ministry. If people are too busy, consider creating special roles for them, such as an advisory panel or a consulting role.

- *Are there churches or other organizations in your area that you can partner with in your ministry?* You should not be doing this work alone. Disaster response is a community effort, and a disaster ministry is an opportunity to become an active participant in serving the community alongside others. Find out what other churches are doing and if there is a niche or special need you might fill. Contact your local emergency management agency office to learn who is coordinating work with churches.

The bottom line is that, whenever possible, it is best to integrate a disaster ministry into things you already do. This leverages your experience, introduces some creative variety that can increase interest among people in existing ministries, allows you to avoid duplication of ministry and leadership, and overall leads to better planning. Also, be careful not to overstretch—be realistic about what your church's role might be in a disaster. In some ways, it's a lot like exercising. As a psychologist, I've worked with numerous clients in the past who set lofty New Year's

goals, only to find that they have set the bar so high there is no way to obtain their goals. They quickly become discouraged and give up. We have seen similar patterns with churches who set unrealistic disaster ministry goals. Remember, start small and build upon the successes you have.[6]

Step 3: Develop a Continuity of Ministry and Operations Plan

In developing a Continuity of Ministry and Operations Plan (COMOP), you are setting the foundation for how your church will continue to operate and begin the recovery process when disaster strikes. Remember, we are starting with a premise that the church is to serve as an example of the kingdom of God through the quality and character of its relationships and service to others. Further, disaster ministry is not just about responding to the disaster-specific events, but it is also about raising the ante, so to speak, on all of our ministries. Making sure that your church is able to function and move forward, even when a disaster strikes, is in itself of great value. Before we can engage in possible specialized emergency responses, we must be able to be the church. That is, we have found that people turn to the church for hope, faith and meaning in addition to practical help after a disaster strikes.[7] Thus, if a church's primary role in their community is not restored, it will be hard to be able to go that extra mile in providing additional care and aid in times of crisis. Below we walk you through the steps necessary for developing a COMOP.

Conduct a ministry impact analysis. A

ministry impact analysis seeks to predict how a disaster might disrupt normal ministry operations and how these losses might impact your congregation and community. Therefore, conducting a ministry impact analysis will help your leadership team decide which ministries and operations are vital. Most all church ministries and programs are important. But a ministry impact analysis asks you to consider which ministries or programs your church could not do without. Another way of looking at it is to ask what ministries or programs that you provide could your community not do without. These are tough questions, but your answers are essential. Imagine that your church building is completely destroyed in a disaster. You won't be able to operate as you always have; you will have to adapt. This means making tough decisions about prioritizing essential ministries and programs. It can be helpful to survey, interview or hold group meetings to assist with the prioritization process.

There is a long running joke in academia that if you ask a professor to name the most important class a student can take in college, in most cases the professor will respond with a class that he or she teaches. Having worked as a former youth minister, I have seen similar trends among church leaders. We all believe that what we are working on is essential. Important, probably, but unfortunately, not everything we are working on is essential. To help make this process easier, try to picture what life and ministry will actually be like after a disaster.[8]

I arrived early one morning at a church in Biloxi, Mississippi, about two months after Katrina to interview a local minister for a study I was working on. After the pastor led me into his office he said, "Stay as long as you want, Son. Because as soon as you leave someone else will come in. And when they get up, someone else will be in that chair." About that time the phone rang, and he answered. Then I heard another phone ring, and he pulled out a cell phone. Then I heard another cell phone. This time he pulled out the phone and mouthed, "It's my wife, could you step out?" After I came back in he explained that his office phone and church cell phone were ringing all the time and that he had to get a third phone just so his family could reach him. Imagine you are that pastor. What ministries, in that moment, would you see as essential to the life of your church and community?

Document recovery strategies. Once you have prioritized your essential ministries, the next step is to allocate resources to ensure you can actually keep the essentials operating when faced with adversity. For example, does one of your essential ministries require a building to carry out activities? What if that building is wiped out? Then you need to make a backup plan for a possible temporary meeting space. You should also identify gaps in resources (goals without a matching resource) and describe steps to address each gap. For instance, does your church have supplies designated solely for use during an emergency? To address gaps, then you need to identify current congregation and community resources that could be leveraged in times of disaster.

A common mistake many churches make is underinsuring their property and assets. Make sure you have your insurance policy up-to-date. You might also reach out to other churches like we've recommended and ask them to be prepared to bring building supplies and volunteers if needed. If your church is part of a denomination or association you might check in about what types of resources are typically available in emergency situations. I did a study of a large denomination's response to Hurricane Katrina (see chapter nine case study). Many of the clergy of this denomination assumed their denomination had funds set aside for rebuilding. However, though the denomination had emergency funds available, these funds were primarily only available for disaster ministry and programming needs. As a result, because of many of the assumptions made about resources that would be available to them from their denomination, most of these churches were underprepared.

When considering liability, you want to make sure you have the right kind of insurance. Less than two months after Katrina my research team was going door-to-door surveying survivors. We came across a house that was still standing but largely gutted out. It caught my attention because I noticed there was a power pole with what looked like a still active power line and a large tree crisscrossed over this person's home—just teetering—and it appeared like either one could give way and fall on the home at any time. I asked a neighbor why the person living there hadn't allowed anyone to remove this disaster waiting to happen that was hovering over his roof.

The neighbor said that his homeowner's insurance company blamed the damage on the flooding instead of the wind and wouldn't cover the damage yet. He added, "He's waiting for one of those things to fall on the house, hoping that somebody will help pay for it." We are not endorsing this approach, but use it to show how important it is to make sure you have the right kind of insurance policies, such as flood insurance (if that's a potential threat), which may require a separate policy or rider.

When documenting recovery strategies, it is also important to take into account that the degree of impact to your congregation and community will affect your church operations. Up to this point, we have encouraged you to think about how your church supports the community. Here, though, we are asking you to consider how the community supports the church. In the same denominational study I just mentioned, I found several churches that had not thought about what would happen when the majority of their congregation was displaced (many had to relocate to other communities) from the community for several months, some for over a year, and others never returned. In these cases the average weekly attendance plummeted. Giving had come to almost a complete stop as people struggled to make their own ends meet. Yet the demand for help and engagement from the community had never been higher. Could your church operate if weekly giving significantly dropped in your church? How might you plan for this? Most of the clergy I interviewed who were able to weather this financial hardship received operating costs assistance from other churches or their denomination. This often meant that either they or another church leader regularly sent out newsletters or spoke to other churches to share their story and to seek ongoing financial assistance until they were able to get back on their feet.

Plan development. After you have documented how your church will sustain essential ministry functions, it is time to develop specialized plans that go beyond sustaining critical operations. Start by creating plans for how your church can adapt essential ministries you identified earlier so that they meet disaster needs. Remember, it is much harder to develop something new than it is to adapt what you are already doing, so this is a good place to start. Once you have created plans for adapting your essential ministries, the next step is to create plans for emergency scenarios your church may not have focused on in the past but may arise in the future.

Plan to adapt existing ministries for disasters. Consider the following examples and questions to help you think about how a church might develop specialized plans by adapting existing ministries.

If your congregation provides Meals on Wheels to shut-ins, consider going the extra step to ask what will happen to them when disaster strikes. Can they evacuate from their homes? Where will they get medications? Does anyone know to check on them? Asking those questions raises the ante for your Meals on Wheels, not in a way that finds fault with the meals program, but in a way that sees new opportunities for serving those who are vulnerable.

Do you run a school? How will parents get connected to their children when disaster strikes? You probably have a disaster plan for your school—most states require that, so get to work if you do not!—but does it distinguish types of disasters? What about a pandemic that requires the school to be closed for two weeks? What will those working parents do? Can you operate an emergency short-term daycare program?

Do you have refugees in your community? Maybe you hold English classes for immigrants and refugees. Perhaps they come from countries where there are no government services or the government cannot be trusted. Do they know what a first responder looks like and why they are at the door? Do they know what a tornado siren sounds like? What happens to them if they are poor (not all refugees are poor) and the local food pantry is flooded?

Create plans for emergency scenarios. The next step is to develop plans for specific emergency scenarios that might arise in a disaster. For starters, create a plan to protect information technology capabilities. Our congregations and communities rely on technology more and more as a means for connecting. Most people and organizations rely more heavily on electronic means for maintaining records and information as hard and physical data is used less. Examples of possible actions are inventorying and documenting all systems, backing up systems and processing facilities, creating contact lists and physically securing your computer assets. Overall, you should take steps to protect, back up and diversify technologies used to support critical ministry processes.

You'll want to create a crisis communication plan that outlines how the congregation will communicate with all of the individuals who are directly or indirectly affected by the disaster. Identifying a way to inform your congregation that an event is happening and what to do in response is one of the first steps to take. For example, if people have to be evacuated from the building, what will be used to communicate—cell phones, text messages, radios or intercoms? Plan how to communicate with families, community members and the media. In most cases, it's helpful to use multiple approaches as some communications go down. If you consider the example used to introduce the chapter, the church's approach to crisis communication was built on the way they already tended to communicate. It can be helpful to write a sample template message in advance so that messages do not have to be composed during the confusion and chaos of the event. It's a good idea to share your disaster plan ahead of time with your congregation so they know how the church plans on functioning after a disaster. Lastly, consider how you might communicate if technology all goes down (cell phone towers destroyed, power lines down, etc.). One church I came across after Hurricane Katrina in New Orleans had two large pieces of particleboard they had recovered from the debris. On one of the pieces of particleboard the church leadership spray-painted upcoming meeting times and locations. On the other piece of particleboard church members would write and nail messages they wanted to communicate with each other.

You may want to develop an evacuation plan that details how you will help people leave the building if a disaster strikes while a service or program is happening. Moving to an open lot near the church may be sensible if a fire of short duration occurs, but the same location may not work if the fire continues for an extended period of time. An evacuation plan should identify existing emergency shelter locations or backup locations that would function as emergency shelters. Churches should negotiate or reconfirm plans for using these spaces at the start of every year. Weather conditions should be part of the plan, allowing for contingencies such as rain, snow, and extreme cold and heat. This plan should also identify transportation options, particularly for those with limited mobility. A reverse evacuation plan—to return people inside the building if an event occurs outside—should also be outlined. Once people are safely inside, a lockdown might be needed.

A lockdown plan might be created to help protect your congregation should a crisis occur like disruptive intruder, domestic dispute or active shooter situation. A lockdown may also be called for when there is a crisis inside and movement within the building will put congregants in jeopardy. In this case, all exterior doors should be locked, and congregation members and staff should stay in the building and lock or obstruct room doors for further protection. In these instances, windows may also need to be covered to help hide people inside from the threat.

A "shelter in place" plan can be made for when there is not time to evacuate or when it may be harmful to leave the building. Church members and staff are held in the building, and windows and doors are closed to protect against exposure and/or debris. These plans might involve opening up your church as a shelter to congregation members and community members who have been displaced by the disaster. One of the easiest ways to do this is to reach out to your local chapter of the Red Cross. If you are willing to allow Red Cross to use your facilities, they will bring in all the equipment that is needed to run an effective shelter, such as cots and blankets. They will even help train your congregation members and church leadership and offer logistic assistance with running a shelter. Further, they will assume liability for any challenges that might happen and help with repairs if any damage occurs from allowing your facility to be used as a shelter. You might also consider opening up your church as a resting place for first responders to be able to regroup and recharge.

Work on specialized disaster ministry plans. In the last chapter we talked about three overarching disaster ministry models. Up to this point the plans we have encouraged you to contemplate largely fall under the disaster-informed ministry model, focusing on what your church already does and embedding disaster ministry into those existing programs. For churches looking to do more, to go beyond your current ministries, here is where you plan for it. Perhaps your church will make a plan for developing a feeding ministry that could be used to care for those in your community or even be deployed to other regions. Another common specialized

ministry you could plan for is equipping a team of volunteers to help with rebuilding homes or clearing debris.

Your specialized disaster ministry plan might be with other churches. I helped with a grant project in Mississippi that led to a disaster chaplain network. Several churches came together to provide psychological first-aid training for clergy and lay leaders. Each of these volunteers signed and agreed to adhere to a set of ethical principles. They went through a background screening process. Letters of recommendation were needed that spoke to their capacity to deal with the challenges of providing disaster care. When Hurricane Gustav threatened, one of my colleagues working on the grant was actually in the emergency operations center in the bunker along the coast ready to take orders from the emergency director to engage the network. I was on the ground ready to relay these orders and ready to supervise the network response. Overall, the possibilities for developing a specialized disaster ministry are endless (see the next chapter for some additional recommendations on how to help other communities affected by disasters).[9]

Foster individual and family disaster plans. To help with developing individual and family disaster plans, you can find information at your local emergency management agency and/or health department, and also online by organizations such as FEMA (e.g., the FEMA resource _Be Aware, Get Prepared, Take Action_).[10] The more prepared your congregation members are, the more resilient your church will be when faced with disaster. Your church might encourage congregation members to do the following:

- Make a "Go-Kit"
- Decide upon a postdisaster meeting place
- Make special needs known
- Develop a disaster communication plan
- Obtain proper insurance
- Set aside emergency funds
- Create an evacuation plan
- Create a family disaster plan

We recognize that many of your congregation members may not have extra income or the financial ability to spend money on preparedness activities. Perhaps your church might plan on ways to help them get ready. Further, if you do an Internet search for preparedness on a budget, you'll find lots of links and videos that can help people get started no matter their financial circumstances. Also consider distributing preparedness educational materials (e.g., checklists) during services or making them available at a resource center. It can also be helpful to make plans to regularly include messaging about the importance of preparedness in email, service and website updates and news.

Step 4: Test and Practice Your Plan

To bring the planning phase full circle, you need to actually put your plan into action. Testing and practicing your plan is a critical step in disaster planning. David sometimes shares a true story that highlights the importance of practicing our plans. Many years ago there was a small troop of soldiers doing survival training who got lost

in a military training drill in a mountainous region. They had all but lost hope and were trying to make peace with the fact that this might be it for them. About that same time one of them found a map of the mountains. So the troop rallied around the map and worked together, eventually finding their way out of the mountains and back to their base camp. It was not until they arrived back at camp, though, that they realized the map was of the wrong mountain range. Plans are just part of the equation to successful church preparedness. If they are not practiced, then you just have a piece of paper. Plans should be like the map illustrated in this story, successfully bringing people together. The true test of a plan is not what is written down (though it does help when it is the right plan!). Rather, the usefulness of a plan can be measured by how well it brings people together to work collaboratively when times are difficult. Here we will provide some training recommendations and examples to help you test your plan.

Prepare your congregation's staff. Staff members should be introduced and become familiar with the church's preparedness activities upon hiring. I was at lunch with a friend who introduced me to a couple of his pastors who happened to be eating at the same restaurant. My friend shared with them a little about my role at HDI. One of the pastors said that he would like to talk with me about helping their church develop a plan. The other pastor quickly jumped in and said, "We already have one, we developed it about five years ago." Though a plan had been developed, it was clear from this exchange that not all the staff knew about it. Church staff should be informed and also receive ongoing training regarding their disaster-related roles, as well as their specific job function during times of disaster.

Use exercises to practice and validate your plans. Drills and exercises should be conducted to validate emergency response, ministry continuity and crisis communications plans and to evaluate the ability of the disaster ministry team and congregation members to carry out their assigned roles and responsibilities. Doing this will help you identify possible gaps or missing parts in your plans. One helpful way to practice your plan is to create a hypothetical incident that your team or church will practice responding to. For example, you might develop a tabletop exercise. A tabletop exercise is discussion based; participants converse about their various roles during an emergency and specific responses to particular situations. This exercise presents a scenario to the team(s) and then allows the team to discuss the steps that their area(s) of responsibility executes in response to the scenario in order to recover and resume the functions for which they are responsible. A facilitator guides participants through a consideration of various contingencies. You might also consider actually role-playing a specific situation or emergency.

I was recently consulting with a church that wanted help developing a plan for an active shooter scenario. After working to develop the plan I asked that the church's disaster ministry team practice the plan. After a meeting they all worked to huddle everyone together in a safe and secure backroom with no windows. The senior pastor then walked from room to room to check if everyone had followed the plan. He found that they had executed the plan perfectly except for one major flaw. They had chosen the most removed and isolated room just as instructed. However, when the pastor jiggled the doorknob, the door swung wide open. You see, the room they chose met all the criteria set forth in their plan, but they had overlooked the fact that the room did not have a lock on the door. Plans need to be practiced to see how your disaster ministry team and congregation actually respond. Practicing will also help you identify challenges and areas that may need to be changed. Practicing helps transfer knowledge into capabilities.

Beware of Planning

Up to this point we have been emphasizing making plans for everything. Before we end, we want to add a word of caution. Plans can be dangerous! Plans can create the impression of being prepared when in fact you are not prepared. Being prepared is about people knowing what they need to do and having the training and support they need in order to do it. Using the example of dealing with a disruptive person during a service, if we create a plan and put it on file with the church office but do not train both new and experienced ushers, then we are no better prepared than we were without the plan. We may in fact be worse off because we could be lulled into thinking we are prepared when we are not and be unaware of the problem.

This begs the basic question, What does it mean to be prepared? If the goal is preparedness, then planning is an important step, but only a step. Moving from a plan to being prepared can be addressed in a series of questions:

1. Who will be the champion of the plan, making sure that it is kept current and relevant, updating it as needed?

2. Who will be required to act on the plan, and are they ready and able? If it is an evacuation plan, who will call for the evacuation and who will be needed to help people evacuate? What knowledge or skills do they need, and how will the responsible people get those skills?

3. As people come and go, or as people forget their training, how will you make sure that people stay prepared? Will you do exercises? Will you incorporate brief updates into committee meetings (i.e., institute "five minutes to prepare" sometime during every meeting of deacons)?

4. Finally, who will keep track of what has been done and what continues to be done? People come and go, and when key people leave, part of the church's "memory" leaves with them. Creating a record preserves what has been done and helps those who are new to learn and build upon your work.

Conclusion

Your disaster plan is a living document—it should be updated and revised based on the exercise results and church leadership's recommendations. Conducting a risk assessment will help you become more aware of the possible threats facing your church and will help you develop more targeted

plans. The COMOP will help you prioritize and get ready for how you will actually carry out your disaster ministry. The training and exercises we recommended can be used to improve the plan by determining the parts of the plan that require improvement and by making the changes. Revise the plan as needed to reflect changes in operations and staff and to fix problems discovered during testing. This should occur at least annually, but circumstances could provoke more frequent updates. It can also be helpful to provide or identify initial and refresher training opportunities for church leadership and congregation members in preparedness and emergency responsibilities. Overall, the take-home point of the chapter should be that plans are a useful tool to enhance preparedness. But more important, it is what your team does with the plan that really matters.

Discussion Questions

1. What are the most probable risks in your area? If you are unsure, check with your local FEMA office. Are you surprised by the answer?

2. Make a template for a disaster plan and a kit list for disaster supplies. What did you learn about cost and effort as you did this? Would the cost make this kit out of reach for some members of your church? How will you assist with that?

3. If your church building is destroyed, where would you meet? Are essential documents protected from fire and flood?

4. Who is the "champion" for the plans you create? What does your champion need from the church in order to be successful?

chapter six

Response

The case study presented in this section, written by Catherine McNiel and lightly edited for publication here, describes how one church stepped up to help its community.[1]

At 9:45 a.m. on Sunday, November 4, 2012, the second worship service at Wheaton Bible Church was just beginning. A few miles down the road at Timber Lake Apartments (located in a predominantly Hispanic neighborhood), Juana and Jose Rangel were asleep in their third-floor apartment, having worked the graveyard shift the night before. Their son, ten-year-old Christopher, heard the baby crying and woke his mother, Juana, to feed him. As Christopher left his parents' room, he heard screaming and shouting: "Fire!" He ran to the balcony, expecting to see a fire in the distance. Instead, he was shocked to see the balcony adjacent to his own was ablaze. He dashed back inside and frantically alerted his family. Afraid the apartment might explode, the family ran for safety. "I was in shock," Juana said. "As I saw how my apartment was burning, I was crying and crying." Juana, who is diabetic, literally did go into shock and was taken by ambulance to the hospital.

The damage was extensive. The fire destroyed all the units in the building; most of the contents were considered a total loss. The following hours and days were critical for the nearly one hundred people who were displaced, in shock and grieving. The majority of these families had very few resources before the disaster, and had even fewer afterward. For many of the survivors language was a barrier, which added to their vulnerability and made communication more difficult. Many were recent immigrants who relied on cash and paper documents kept in their homes. Those affected were quickly surrounded by members of the fire and police departments, representatives of Timber Lake management, volunteers and staff from Wheaton Bible Church (WBC) and Iglesia del Pueblo (WBC's Hispanic congregation), the Puente del Pueblo team (WBC's onsite ministry initiative at Timber Lake), staff from Outreach Community Center, and Red Cross workers. Representatives of the City of West Chicago, DuPage County and the School District 33 were also involved.

Together they worked to provide for the most immediate needs. The evening of the fire all families affected by it had a safe place to stay, either with friends and family or in a local motel, paid for by the Red Cross and arranged by Northridge Holdings, an apartment referral service. The next day, the relief teams had delivered basic provisions to each family, and Timber Lake had arranged for most of the families to lease a new apartment in the complex or in other properties they managed. Puente del Pueblo began assessing specific longer-term needs, including furniture and document replacement.

The people of Wheaton Bible Church and others in the community responded with an outpouring of donations, and a "store" was set up in the community center where residents could "shop" for the items that would most meet their individual needs. Over fifty volunteers from WBC and Iglesia del Pueblo responded to assist. One of Puente's roles in the days after the fire was to facilitate effective communication between the fire survivors and the various agencies and departments offering assistance. Meetings were held to provide meals and to discuss the actions being taken and expectations for the coming days. One of the most pressing questions the nearly one hundred displaced residents had was whether or not they would be allowed access to their apartments to retrieve any belongings that had survived. Many people didn't have their wallets, car keys, important papers, daily medications or shoes.

Susan, a resident, shared that rebuilding your life takes time and money, and timely, sensitive help is so needed. She believes that in this respect she and her neighbors

were very fortunate, pointing out that it really did take a village to get this job done. "It was such a tremendous effort between WBC, Puente del Pueblo and the Timber Lake management office. They coordinated their efforts for the families who really needed assistance." Right after the fire, she said, "We were all the same, sitting with what we had with us—and that's all. It didn't matter what backgrounds we had. Puente was the arm of WBC, and together with Timber Lake management office they went above and beyond in getting us to a motel for the first night and then into new apartments. They fought to give us extra time to retrieve our things from our homes. Seeing this experience unfold gave us a compelling reason to attend WBC." She and her boyfriend had not attended before the fire but now attend the worship service and have visited several of the adult communities. She added, "It is important for the WBC community to know the value of what they did. They mobilized quickly to do a huge job. The leadership said what they needed and the people of the church did what they could. It meant a lot to the families. It meant a lot to us. Sometimes important things go unsaid, but it is important to know we appreciated it. They treated us like family—with a 'warm hug' level of involvement."

She was amazed by people like Carlos who came out on a Saturday morning to help strangers and said they were happy to do it. "They didn't do it for the credit but for God," she added. "That's why we decided to attend WBC. It was amazing. And if an English Bible study starts up at the clubhouse, we'll be there." The impact of

Christ's body working together was felt not only by those who lost their homes but also by the other agencies that responded. A Red Cross staffer approached Matthew McNiel, director of Puente del Pueblo, the night after the incident and said, "This is amazing. You guys are a church? We never see this kind of response. It is so fantastic, the way you are responding to this crisis." Later, a public-relations representative for the DuPage County Office of Homeland Security and Emergency Management also approached Matthew to share how astonished everyone was to see a church and social-service agency (Puente del Pueblo and Outreach Community Ministries) working together so effectively. One of the main reasons this effort was so effective was because WBC staff and volunteers had been intentional in getting to know the other organizations mentioned and fostering those relationships. This allowed for all parties to work together quickly and collaboratively.

The managers of the Timber Lake Apartments also sent a letter to the church and the church leaders that helped with the response, which read:

Words cannot express the blessing that you have been to the management and residents of Timber Lake Apartments. While the fire was still burning, and we were attending to the shock and despair of the residents of the 24 apartments—who left their apartments with just the clothes on their back—I was receiving phone calls from your ministry offering your help. Within a couple of hours, you sent food and emailed 1,600 people requesting help for our residents. I saw a picture of the storeroom in your church six hours after the email went out, filled with clothes and supplies. Each person in each family was given seven changes of clothing and then the leftovers were distributed to whoever needed them. It was like the five loaves and two fish that were multiplied and distributed in order to meet the needs of the people.

It was a great testimony of the outpouring of God's love, not only through words, but through your actions. Even the Mayor, Chief of Police, Fire Chief and the Red Cross all individually said that they had never seen anything like the help and care that was given to the victims.

During the next week, the Wednesday night Bible study that you conduct at Timber Lake cooked several evening meals for all of the residents in the fire. You also provided help and trained counselors to assist and wipe the tears from their eyes and sustain them on the days they were able to go back into the building and retrieve whatever personal belongings they could salvage from the debris.

Many times we thank God for the mysterious way that God has orchestrated his plan with your ministry at Timber Lake Apartments.

The love of God, through you, shines at Timber Lake Apartments and the rest of the Village of West Chicago!

Purpose

The disaster response phase is devoted to steps to take during and immediately following a disaster. The purpose of this chapter is to walk you through a critical series of common response actions that you and your congregation may be called upon to carry out in the immediate aftermath of a disaster striking your community. Specifically, we focus on implementing your disaster ministry plan as well as three common response activities, including crisis communication, sheltering and evacuation, and protecting property.

Implementing Your Disaster Ministry Plan

You have worked hard pulling together your disaster ministry team and planning. Imagine that a disaster is threatening or that your community has just been hit by a disaster. Now is the time to put all that hard work you've invested in developing a disaster ministry into action. This section summarizes some general principles for implementing your disaster ministry plan.

Foster transparency with your congregation. When a crisis is ongoing, church leaders need to come across as calm, competent and sober to persuade people of the gravity of the circumstances and the suitability of the instructions being provided. The disaster ministry team will build confidence and the trust of the congregation by being transparent about their work and letting people know who they are and what they do. One of the best ways to do this is to have one member of the team who assumes responsibility for telling the church and, if appropriate, the community about the work of the team. Get up in front of the church on Sunday morning and explain who you are and why you are doing this, and most importantly, why this ministry is an expression of the mission of the church. As you develop plans or hold training sessions, be public about it and even invite others to contribute their ideas. When people see something developing, and even more so, when they make a contribution, there is a growing sense of ownership.

Assess and respond immediately. Following the plan starts with having clear criteria about what triggers the plan—that is, what kind of events call for putting the plan into action. Obviously you cannot hold a committee meeting during a crisis, so some people need to be empowered and trusted to call for a response. The disaster ministry coordinator and disaster ministry team will need to make a very quick but careful assessment of the situation. Determine whether a disaster exists and, if so, the type of crisis, the location and the magnitude. Once the initial defensive steps are taken, you can collect more information to determine further responses. If there is indeed a disaster, immediately determine what basic action is necessary and carry it out promptly. The capacity to make a rapid, fitting response is based on having a plan with precisely determined roles and duties along with training and practice. With proper training, the disaster ministry team, staff, leadership and congregants will be more likely to respond promptly and appropriately.[2]

Notify appropriate emergency responders and the disaster ministry team. One frequently made mistake is to wait to call emergency responders (e.g., police or fire departments). When a disaster is ongoing, people often think it can be dealt with in-house. But it is better to be overly cautious and call emergency responders to the scene, even if the situation has been taken care of when they arrive. To put off calling is to risk further injury and damage. Having emergency responders arrive to discover a fire put out is better than having them arrive too late to stop injuries to people or property. During a situation, unless told otherwise, the disaster ministry team members should follow through with their appointed responsibilities.

Common Response Activities

No disaster plan, regardless of how complete, can prepare for every event that can come up during a catastrophe. Spending a great deal of time and effort on a disaster plan should not prevent the disaster ministry team from recognizing that some surprises and accompanying confusion will always come up in the event of a disaster. However, though we may not be able to predict every need that will arise, we have found that being prepared to perform certain tasks will help your church be more resilient—as well as better positioned to respond to unexpected challenges. These core tasks include engaging in crisis communication, assisting with evacuation and sheltering, and protecting property. Because these are common tasks many congregations must perform in a disaster, we will take a closer look at each one.

Crisis communication. When a disaster occurs, the need to communicate is immediate. If ministry operations are interrupted, congregation and community members will need to be informed of how it will affect them. During a disaster, use the channels of communication identified in the plan. As we write elsewhere, "Congregation members and their families will be concerned and want information.

Neighbors living near the facility may need information—especially if they are threatened by the incident. All of these groups will want information before the congregation has a chance to begin communicating. An important component of the preparedness program is the crisis communication."[3] The disaster ministry team should communicate regularly with staff and volunteers who are managing survivors. Deprived of prompt and correct information, the safety plan cannot be carried out in the event of a disaster. Further information concerning assembly and shelter procedures may also be needed, based on the plan or the team working on the disaster.

Gather contact information. Contact information needs to be compiled in advance and stored so that it will be immediately accessible during an incident. Be sure to collect possible alternative and emergency contact information as well. You likely already have contact information for clergy, church leadership and membership, which may be exported from the church's databases. Include as much information for each contact as possible (e.g., organization name, contact name, business telephone number, cell number, fax number and email address). Update lists on a regular basis, and ensure that they protect confidential information and can only be accessed by authorized users, or are kept in a backup location for the crisis communications team. Electronic lists can also be hosted on a secure server for remote access with a web browser. Hard copies of lists should be available at the alternate location.[4]

Develop scripts for possible disaster sce-narios. It can be helpful to develop scripted messages before a disaster hits to have ready to use when responding to a catastrophe. For example, you might provide information about the seriousness of a potential threat, or possibly convey information about if, when and where services will take place if a disaster hits. Writing messages during an incident can be difficult as a result of the pressures imposed in a disaster scenario. Therefore, it is best to script message templates in advance if possible. Pre-scripted messages should be prepared using information developed during the risk assessment process. This will help you identify scenarios that would require communications with the congregation and community. You can write messages in advance as templates, adding details pertinent to the actual disaster later. The management team can create and approve pre-scripted messages and store them such that they will be accessible when they become necessary.

Identify communication methods. If you have advance warning of a disaster, such as in the case of an approaching hurricane, you should take steps to communicate and provide warnings for your congregation and possibly community. Be sure to consider those in your church and community that you previously identified as high risk for this type of event, and take extra precautions to make sure their needs are addressed. Unfortunately, not all disasters give advance warning. Thus, your disaster ministry team needs to determine how congregation leadership will communicate with one another and the congregation in the event standard communication methods become unavailable for an extended period of time. Prior to the occurrence of a disaster, make a plan for where staff will meet if the church becomes unavailable as a result of a sudden disaster. Alternative communication methods should be available in case normal channels are not. Examples of common crisis communication strategies include:

- Call-down procedure (e.g., activate "prayer chain") text messaging

- Text broadcasting

- Social media updates

- Alternate call-in number of region (perhaps with a sister church)

- Cloud documents (e.g., leaving messages on Google Docs)

Perhaps your church is small and may not have access to some of these technologies for communicating. Many local and regional emergency management agencies have notification services the community can sign up for to receive things like emergency alerts. In this case, you could encourage your members to take advantage of these types of free services.[5]

Sheltering and evacuation. A few years ago I was visiting a church in the greater Chicago area when a severe storm went through and caused significant wind damage. During the service the electricity went off. Mild panic broke out among many of the members because they feared a tornado. Rather than addressing what was happening, the church leadership kept the service going without providing any instructions! Many of the parents immediately went to check on their children. Some people left the service and headed to the basement. Others left briskly for their vehicles, though the roads were blocked and there were power lines down near the church. Fortunately no one was injured. Things could have been much worse. Overall, this example highlights the need for churches to be ready to facilitate sheltering and evacuation activ-

whether there is immediate danger. If you see large amounts of debris in the air, or if local authorities say the air is badly contaminated, you may want to take this kind of action. The process used to seal the room is considered a temporary protective measure to create a barrier between you and potentially contaminated air outside. Ten square feet of floor space per person will provide sufficient air to prevent carbon di-

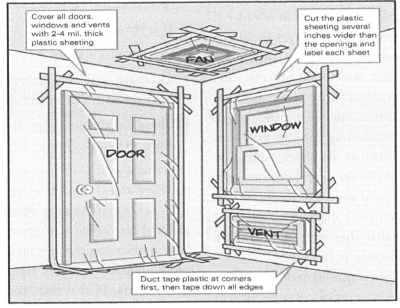

Figure 6.1[6]

ities. Next we discuss different ways to shelter in the event that a disaster strikes while your church is in service, as well as evacuation guidelines.

Shelter in place. If there is a disaster or the potential for one while people are in the church, they may need to stay inside and construct a barrier against possible hazards outside. Using common sense and any information you have, evaluate the situation and make a determination as to

oxide build-up for up to five hours, assuming a normal breathing rate while resting. But it is unlikely that local officials will encourage people to stay in a sealed room for longer than two to three hours because the capability to prevent contaminants from entering decreases over time. Evacuation will then become the most helpful action to take. Be sure to ventilate the shelter when the hazard has passed to prevent breathing contaminated air still inside.

Temporary shelter. The above scenario assumes a disaster strikes while people are in your church. Temporary shelter, on the other hand, occurs when your church takes people in from the community. For example, people from another community may be ordered by local officials to evacuate, and some will turn to churches for temporary shelter. In other cases, your community may be hit hard by a disaster and people find themselves without places to live and are therefore in need of temporary shelter. As much as possible, plan ahead to ensure a safe and secure place for those you may shelter, as well as those who call your church their spiritual home. Following are some basic steps for preparing your congregation to provide temporary shelter, provided by Brotherhood Mutual.[7]

- Determine first how many people your facility can handle. Fire codes and local ordinances set the number of people that can be in your facility at one time.

- Limit the areas of your facility in which refugees will have access.

- Enlist capable members of your congregation to minister and monitor activities of the people you house in your building on a 24/7 basis. Conduct regular patrols in areas accessible to disaster survivors.

- Record the names of everyone you shelter. Also ask for the names of relatives to contact in the event of an emergency.

- Establish procedures to address emergencies. Be prepared to handle minor first-aid issues. Ensure that everyone in the shelter is aware of your emergency plan, especially ministry workers from your congregation.

- Establish procedures to address any unlawful activities that may occur within your church facility. Communicate these procedures to those you house and to members of your congregation who are helping. You also may want to consider hiring specialists to help with security.

- Determine how you will handle weapons and valuables that disaster survivors may have in their possession when they enter your shelter. Those you help should not be allowed to possess weapons of any kind while they are housed at your church. Consider using a safe or tightly secured room to safeguard valuables. Before doing so, consider your legal responsibilities and the insurance risks you may incur while securing items for disaster survivors.

- Secure and/or monitor entrances at all times. Make sure the interior doors are in good repair and unlocked in areas where disaster survivors may have access.

- Determine if food will be prepared onsite or brought in from the outside. The size of your church kitchen, if it has one, and local health department regulations will drive your ability to serve food in your facility.

- Establish how you will maintain sanitary conditions. Can you provide shower facilities for both men and women? Consider the accumulation of trash and garbage. Maintain and perhaps increase janitorial services or seek additional volunteers.

- Monitor the condition of your building on an ongoing basis. Make repairs promptly when needed, especially those that correct health and safety hazards.

- Ensure that your facility is properly lighted.

- Strongly encourage parents to be responsible for the safety of their children.

- Have volunteers screened, including background checks.

- Install safety devices on all electrical outlets in areas where children may be housed.

- Ensure that age-appropriate toys are provided to children. Be aware of toys that have small parts or work in ways that may cause injury to children.

- Inspect your playground equipment, if applicable, and repair it if necessary. Adult supervisors should always be present while children are playing. Keep sidewalks cleared of toys and other obstacles that may cause falls and other injuries.[8]

There are also some special considerations you should address. Ensure that your church's volunteers, especially those responsible for security, are qualified to recognize potential sex offenders and victims of abuse. If any concerning incidents occur, or if abuse is suspected or occurs within the church shelter, contact local law enforcement officials immediately. We recommend limiting those who are involved in events in which children are present to people you know from your ministry and those who have had background checks in advance, especially when children are separated from their parents or are participating in group activities. As we noted during the planning chapter, consider working with an established group like the American Red Cross to help you better be equipped for these types of activities, or consult with local emergency management and authorities to ensure you are operating within local ordinances and laws.[9]

Evacuating your congregation during a service. Disaster plans often describe how to get ready for a disaster but lack basic information about how to evacuate. To evacuate congregation members in a timely manner necessitates a warning system that can be heard throughout the building. Check the fire alarm system to find out whether it can be heard by all. If the building does not have a fire alarm system, use a public address system or a viable alternative to warn people to evacuate. Use the evacuation signal during drills so that people will be able to recognize the sound. Ensure that sufficient exits are always available. Keep a list of congregation members and use a visitor log in the reception area or main office. Appoint someone to bring the lists to the assembly area when the building is evacuated. Use the lists to count heads and tell emergency responders whether anyone is missing. If a warning is given to congregation members, be sure to do the following:

- Assign an evacuation team leader and specific employees to direct evacuation of the building.

- Go around the building and confirm that exits are clearly marked as such and that there is enough lighting to travel safely to an exit.

- Remove anything that blocks an exit.

- Direct attendees to an alternate safe exit if an exit is blocked.

- Go into each stairwell, walk down the stairs and open the exit door.

- Go on walking until you reach a safe distance from the building.

- Determine whether this safe area is an appropriate assembly area for evacuees.

- Inform everyone in the church of the need to evacuate the building and/or campus.

- Examine your emergency supply list, making sure all supplies needed are packed in boxes and ready to transport.

- Make sure transportation is available to successfully evacuate everyone.

- Make sure all vehicles being used for transportation have money for tolls and maps to the evacuation destination (if applicable) and that drivers have cell phones.

- Determine the order of evacuation. Try to keep people on each floor or area of a building together to make determining a head count easier.

- Determine if some of the staff or parishioners have relatives who could come and pick them up. This will help those being taken to a shelter feel more comfortable than they would as strangers in a public shelter.

- Be sure the alternative receiving facility has been notified if evacuating to an offsite location.

- Be sure to notify local authorities of imminent evacuation.

- List the names of individuals who will be in charge during an emergency.

- If you are evacuating to a residential facility such as a shelter, if possible, be sure to tell each person to take the following: two to three changes of clothing, one pillow, two blankets, all toiletry articles needed, glasses, hearing aids, medicines and so on.[10]

Encouraging your congregation to evacuate from the community. In some cases local officials will conclude that mandatory evacuations are needed due to the seriousness of the hazards. Other times evacuations are merely advised, or people will decide to evacuate to prevent situations they think could be dangerous. However, there may be members of your congregation who either are not reachable by local officials or may be hesitant to heed the warning of local officials. I had the opportunity to work with some Vietnamese churches following Hurricane Katrina. I learned that many of their members did not have access to many of the technologies we often take for granted, such as Internet access. Further, most of the congregation members were involved in the fishing business. To help notify members, church leaders and volunteers went to the docks to help spread the word and pass out flyers of information.

In my work with the African American church in Mississippi, I learned from several of the pastors that even though there were serious warnings given by local officials about the potential threat of Katrina, many of their members did not trust government officials or were skeptical at best. For the message to be "heard," it had to come from a source members of the church and community trusted. In the churches where the senior pastor passed along the government warnings, people were more receptive to the message and took the warnings more seriously because they heard the information directly from their pastor.

Overall, it's important for you to recognize the possible influence your messaging, especially about evacuation, may have on congregation members. At the onset of the handbook, I shared how my family learned of Katrina by visiting a church near where we lived. What I didn't share in chapter one was that the pastor went on to preach, "If you evacuate, it's because you don't have enough faith in God." Yet, I learned later from a friend attending another church before the storm that his pastor had preached, "If you don't evacuate or at least take precautions, you are putting the Lord your God to the test." I know the message I heard from the pulpit caused a lot of internal conflict for me that morning, and caused me to second-guess how my family and I should prepare. I can only imagine the same was true for others. I chose to evacuate. But I often wonder how many people who had the means and resources to evacuate (I recognize many did not have the ability) stayed because of the sermon that was preached and remained in harm's way.

Protecting church property. Before a disaster strikes there are several things you can do to help prepare your church property for a disaster. Many people along the Mississippi Gulf Coast referred to the Sunday after Hurricane Katrina as "slab Sunday"

because numerous churches were destroyed, leaving only the concrete slab foundation behind. In some situations like this, there may be little that can be done to protect church property. However, there were also numerous churches in the region that were damaged but salvageable, and even others with only minor damage. The fallout and path of destruction caused by disasters can be random. There may be times that despite planning and mitigating preparations, no course of action could have prevented property damage. Regardless, you should still take precautions where you can to enhance your property's ability to weather adversity. Jesus was not speaking about the topic at hand in Luke 4:12—"Do not put the Lord your God to the test"—but the truth of those words is very applicable to how we take care of and protect the resources for which we are stewards. We should all prepare to the best of our abilities and resources as though our church will be the one still standing so that we will be better positioned to continue to minister to those around us. In the denominational study I mentioned earlier, I had the opportunity to interview clergy who pastored churches that fit into each of the categories of loss that I just described, from nothing left but the slab to minor damage.[11] In this section, we share some of the lessons learned from these clergy and from others about how to protect your church property.

Perform routine maintenance. We realize that the costs of regular and preventative maintenance may be difficult for some churches, depending on their resources. However, if at all possible, you should try to regularly address maintenance issues as they arise rather than putting them off. When you are sick, if you don't get rest, eat well and perhaps take the necessary medicine, your condition will probably get worse. Whereas, had you taken the proper precautions when you first started not feeling well, you may have been able to prevent the illness from getting worse. Though this may not always be the case, it stacks the odds in your favor. The same can be said when it comes to performing routine maintenance. Performing regular maintenance can help address risks that may seem minor, but when stressed by a disaster can develop into a significant problem. For example, a small crack in a pipe could turn into a busted pipe that floods your basement when your neighborhood's sewer system is overcome by a torrential rain. Had regular maintenance been performed on the pipe, it may not have flooded your basement. Some examples of regular maintenance tasks that should be performed on an annual basis to help keep small problems from turning into potentially big problems after a disaster include trimming trees near rooflines and inspecting the following: roofs, foundations, smoke detectors, HVAC equipment, wiring, power connection, circuit boxes, water heaters, gutters and drains. More regular maintenance might also include checking security canopies and covered walks, emergency supplies, and vehicular issues if applicable. By no means is this a comprehensive list, but it should help you get started.

Also, keep in mind that there may be other steps that you can take to protect your church property. For example, if your church is located in a hurricane or tornado area, there are standards for securing buildings. The same thing is true for communities located in flood areas or near the ocean. If your church has the means, you might also follow FEMA's guidelines for developing a community safe room.[12]

Reduce risk of unnecessary damage. One of the pastors I interviewed shared about going to his church to get some important documents as Hurricane Katrina neared. He had just been in the church earlier in the week and felt completely safe. But with this storm on the way, it opened his eyes to all the potential risks and dangers around him. He now saw his unsecured bookshelves along his walls as an avalanche waiting to happen. What he previously saw as small propane tanks stored in the basement for cookouts were now small bombs waiting to go off. After securing these items and several others in the church, he went to wash his hands to clean up before leaving. As the water poured out of the faucet, he had a mental image of the water pouring into the sink, rushing over and throughout the church basement. He realized that he needed to shut off the water main to try and prevent possible water damage. His eyes also opened to other critical issues that needed to be addressed, like shutting off the gas and power main switches.

The following are some FEMA examples of easy-to-implement, low-to-no-cost mitigation steps:

- Remove all debris from culverts, streams and channels to allow the free flow of potential floodwaters.

- Clean storm drains and gutters and remove debris from around the church.

- Move shrubs and other landscaping away from the sides of the building.

- Clear dead brush and grass from the property so that it won't serve as fuel to spread fire.

- Install cabinet locks.

- Secure televisions, computers, or other heavy appliances and equipment with flexible straps.

- Anchor bookshelves and large cabinets to walls.

- Strap water heaters to walls.

- Secure or remove items that could become projectiles in high winds.

- Consider raising water heaters and other appliances to avoid flood damage.[13]

Minimize risk of further damage. The above are ideals and assume that you have time to prepare before the disaster strikes. Unfortunately, we know that we don't always have warning and that disasters can come out of nowhere. Here we focus on returning to your property right after the disaster and steps that you can take to try and minimize further damage to your property. Though you may be anxious to see the condition of your property, do not return to it before local officials have determined the area is safe. Carefully go around the outside and look for loose power lines, gas leaks and structural damage. If there is any doubt about safety, have your facility inspected by a qualified building inspector or structural engineer prior to entering. This may sound unlikely, but also be aware that disaster situations can cause animals to act in unpredictable ways, especially stray or wild animals. I had the unfortunate experience of having just such an encounter on the eve of Halloween after Katrina. I was dragging debris and tree branches out of my backyard to the curb when I heard loose gravel rustling followed by growling. I looked up and, before I could respond, my neighbor's dog attacked me, biting the back of my leg. Fortunately I was able to use one of the tree branches I had dragged out to separate the dog from me, and the dog's owner was outside and immediately interceded. The dog had never attacked anyone before, but had been scared by the hurricane and had accidentally been spooked by the sound of me clearing debris.

Once you have ensured that it is safe to enter your property, you should take any steps you can to prevent further loss or damage. For example, if your roof was damaged but is still largely intact, you might have someone with construction experience from your congregation patch the damaged area with a tarp. This may help prevent additional water or weather damage from harming your church. Likewise, if it is a large-scale disaster that leaves a major path of destruction in its aftermath, you need to be prepared for the fact that it may take the insurance company days, weeks or even months before they can assess your damage. Consequently, as soon as you have phone access and have had a chance to check on your property, you should report your claim. The sooner it is reported, the sooner someone can get out to help.

Ask for advice about what other things

you might do to help prevent damage. I took a group of about ten students to help with flooding that happened in the greater Chicago area a few years ago. We helped gut and muck out several flooded homes. Had we not worked with the homeowners and the church volunteers assisting, there would have likely been even more water damage and even mold issues. However, because we responded right away, we were able to help reduce both. I have unfortunately heard a couple of devastating stories where a church's claim was not fully taken care of because the insurance company said their attempt to make things better actually made them worse. However, these stories are in the minority, and in fact, most insurance companies encourage congregations to take whatever steps they can to prevent further damage. To be safe, we would encourage you to contact your provider before or as soon as you can to get guidance regarding your policy.[14]

Finally, as we noted in the planning chapter, be sure that you have the proper types of insurance, that your policy is up-to-date and that you have enough coverage. One of the things many churches do not realize is that the cost of materials and labor often skyrocket in the immediate aftermath of a disaster. This means it may cost more to rebuild your church, so you'll want to account for this in your policy. Your church may also want to set aside some additional funds in the church budget for the possibility that the cost of insurance goes up. There were places along the coast that experienced almost a 27 percent

hike in insurance premiums after the storm.

Before concluding this section, we want to offer a word of caution. After major disasters most people who come in to help with repairing damage mean well and truly want to help. However, there are also people and companies (sometimes fake companies) that respond in order to take advantage of people, including churches. One pastor I interviewed after Hurricane Katrina said that a construction company offered to repair their church roof but needed payment up front. Long story short, once the money exchanged hands, the construction company never returned. When the church tried to track down the company, they found out that the company was bogus and didn't really exist.

Conclusion

Having a plan in place can make you think you have everything taken care of. Disasters will always surprise us, so no matter how well you prepare—and preparing is critical—you will still have some risk. Learn to live with the paradox: Make a plan that is as complete and thorough as possible, but always assume it is incomplete and that you are still vulnerable. Some disasters will require you to shelter in place or provide temporary shelter. Consider each of the main risks in your area and what would be needed to care for your members in the church. This could include bringing in people who do not have alternatives for shelter, such as during a fire or power outage during extreme weather.

Discussion Questions

1. What existing plans does the church have in place, and how well do you maintain them? This is your planning track record, and if it is not the best, ask yourself how you will improve it.

2. Does your church have a call system? How well does it work? Does it need improvement?

3. Does your church have the facilities for sheltering? Does it have the supplies? How will the supplies be maintained?

chapter seven

Recovery

Superstorm Sandy was one of the worst natural disasters to ever strike the East Coast. It will be remembered as one of the United States' most costly natural disasters. The following case study highlights the work of six churches on the New Jersey coast during the disaster recovery phase.[1] The churches were significantly affected by the storm as Sandy carved a path through their communities. The case study is based on interviews with the clergy who helped lead these churches through the crisis. The clergy were interviewed around ten months after this horrendous storm, and their stories provide insights into how churches responded to the long-term needs of their congregants and community. Subsequent interviews identified additional lessons learned more than a year after the storm first made landfall in the region.

As churches and leaders moved beyond the response phase, they were forced to adapt their roles. The churches became even more involved in shelter/housing assistance as well as employment assistance during the recovery phase. The churches involved in networking, administration and leadership/liaison service remained constant, as did those involved in transportation and relocation assistance. When asked about additional services, one church responded that their role in networking and administration led to the creation of a housing center for work teams traveling in from all over the country. Housing and shelter also continued to drive the efforts of some churches. One pastor described how many families went back to their homes and "normal life" within weeks after the storm, but 25,000 remained homeless. Two pastors and their churches continued to be involved housing people or helping those families get back in their own homes throughout the recovery period. Two other churches transitioned from disaster shelters to lodging facilities for workers who arrived to provide assistance. Both churches also allocated space and helped coordinate teams as they moved in and out of the area.

Networking, administration, management, counseling and advocacy for victims were all mentioned as some of the services expected of pastors during the recovery phase. Pastors provided on-the-ground contacts for agencies sending teams.

In addition, families still struggling in the wake of the superstorm continued to turn to the church for counsel, advice, assistance and information. Pastors struggled to balance these ongoing challenges with the normal expectations of ministry. Thus, in many ways, Superstorm Sandy forced churches and local organizations to work together. All but one of the pastors reported that during this phase they developed ongoing partnerships with other churches. It was unclear how these cooperative efforts emerged, but it was clear that pastors placed a priority on developing them. One pastor shared, "I think that what Sandy did was make all our local churches throw aside their differences and what I am excited about is that it is still going on." Overall, the churches became involved in developing partnerships in order to meet the ongoing needs of recovery.

Pastors shared numerous individual lessons learned during the recovery phase, such as the importance of learning what you can and can't do, recognizing the need for a theological and biblical rationale for what you are doing, and being open to the incredible need for and blessing of networking. Five of the pastors further disclosed a significant lesson they learned: not counting the costs of disaster relief first. They and their churches paid a considerable price. In addition to financial costs, leaders and churches paid heavy physical and emotional prices, struggling with weariness and burnout. Most of the churches suffered attrition as members moved to other areas, churches or ministries. One church closed its doors when the pastor became unable to sustain both min-

istries of pastor and disaster relief leader. Despite the costs, however, not one pastor expressed regrets. One leader expressed his feeling this way: "Who knows what it is going to be in the long term, but it has cost the church finances, talent, energy; it caused friction because where is the pastor, where is the staff, where is my visitation? But in another way I think if I could, would I change anything? I wouldn't change anything. I don't think that there is anything that we did that I would do differently."

Most of the churches acknowledged the lesson learned concerning the ability to adapt in order to meet needs. Each leader gave an account of how their congregation had done this. One small, traditional church shared their discovery of how to obtain grants to help fund the modifications of their facility so it could be used to house work teams. Another leader marveled at how much their church had responded. He shared, "We learned that we could have incredible impact, if we are willing, and we're willing to jump in there and trust and work together to do things that are out of the box."

One year into the relief efforts, these pastors had some significant suggestions on how to be better prepared. A pastor and wife team suggested that any church desiring to be involved in disaster relief management or response first become acquainted with and work with the National Voluntary Organizations Active in Disaster (VOAD). "VOAD is a nonprofit, nonpartisan, membership-based organization that builds resiliency in communities nationwide. It serves as the forum where organizations share knowledge and resources throughout the disaster cycle—preparation, response, recovery and mitigation—to help disaster survivors and their communities."[2] Two churches that had sought to open their doors as shelters recommended seeking certification through the Red Cross prior to a disaster occurrence. Two of the churches also recommended that denominations provide support and coordination for churches responding to a disaster through the district office or at the national level.

Purpose

The purpose of this chapter is to help your disaster ministry be ready to assist your congregation and community with the long process of recovery from disaster. In this chapter we will cover common recovery activities, as well as strategies for how your church can help other congregations and communities. The goal of the recovery phase is to help people rebuild and start to put their lives back together. Focus on the congregants, community members and facilities, and take as much time as needed for recovery.

Common Recovery Activities

It is important to match the way your disaster ministry helps your congregation and community with the specific needs that arise during each disaster stage (e.g., planning, response, recovery). During the recovery phase, you may keep on doing some of the same tasks you did right after the disaster, but the degree to which you engage in these tasks may either ramp up or perhaps slow down. This can be seen in the Superstorm Sandy example at the be-

ginning of this chapter. Following are several common activities that we have found many churches engage in during the recovery phase of the disaster life cycle.

Networking. Some churches may have the volunteers, skilled labor and resources to be able to carry out long-term recovery ministries. However, we found that long-term recovery efforts are more likely successful if churches come together with one another or with other organizations. The needs (e.g., rebuilding, mental health, spiritual struggles) left behind after a disaster can be overwhelming and in most cases are larger than any one church can handle, unless perhaps it is a smaller-scale crisis or emergency. Still, we encourage you to consider how you might collaborate with others.

Start by looking for existing efforts already underway. Check out congregations and faith-based and community organizations already doing good work in your community. Is there an active ministerial association that might be able to take the lead on recovery efforts? There are also some explicitly Christian networks that might be available where you live that you might connect with like the Christian Emergency Network.[3] Many states also have active multifaith disaster groups, for more, see the National Disaster Interfaiths Network.[4] You might also consider joining a state chapter of the National Voluntary Organizations Active in Disaster (NVOAD).[5] The NVOAD consists of major disaster relief organizations, including many Christian organizations. It is a formal network that works closely with FEMA in times of major disasters and helps activate and mobilize local efforts through VOAD state chapters.

We have had hundreds of church leaders from all over the country and across the globe attend our annual Disaster Ministry Conference the last few years.[6] We've observed that many of the church leaders who attend are not familiar with NVOAD or their local or state chapter prior to our conference. Yet, there tend to be a number of church leaders who have helped their congregation through disaster. Time and time again, those who share their disaster experience have reported that getting connected to a local VOAD is one of the best ways to join a community's response to disastrous events. This sentiment has also been widely echoed by many of the national and global experts that we have invited to speak at the conference. A common challenge we have listened to from local churches who have found themselves in the middle of a community impacted by a disaster is that some have been turned away and not allowed to assist with disaster recovery efforts. Getting to know and being known by your local VOAD does not guarantee your congregation will be asked to formally partner in disaster response. However, doing so improves the likelihood that your congregation will be more aware of what organizations are responding, resources available and potential service opportunities. In some places, churches play a vital role in their local VOAD's disaster response as collaborative partners. In other instances churches might be invited to support or volunteer through established member organizations that make up the VOAD. Re-

gardless, if there is a VOAD nearby, it's worth checking into.

We recently visited FEMA national headquarters in Washington, D.C., and it just so happened that the FEMA headquarters was abuzz in preparing for a tropical storm that was headed toward Hawaii. There were hundreds of emergency management professionals seated at computers, on the phones, in meetings and tracking along with weather updates being posted on giant wall-size screens around the room. In addition to emergency managers and representatives from the major branches of the government and military, there were also members of the NVOAD volunteering and present. They were working closely with FEMA and the other organizations represented to help communicate and coordinate with organizations, including churches and faith-based NGOs on the ground.

If there is not an established network or collaborative meetings already underway in your community, then consider taking the lead as the host. You might start by hosting an exploratory meeting where you invite other clergy or congregations together to explore potential collaborations and launch a collaborative network. For example, you might invite people from other nearby congregations or your social network to participate in a discussion about your community, pressing needs and potential solutions. Collaborative meetings often engage people new to service and unclear about next steps. Building community through collaborative meetings is a critical step toward improving your ability to carry out your disaster ministry during the recovery phase.

In the event of a major disaster, it is common for Christian disaster relief organizations to deploy to communities significantly affected to provide aid and organizational support. Many of these service groups have identified community needs and have built the expertise to provide solutions. Thus, you might also consider working with or through one of these groups. Though not an exhaustive list, table 7.1 provides a few examples of Christian disaster relief organizations that you might collaborate with. An overview of many of these organizations can be found in *Prepared to Care: Guide to Disaster Ministry in Your Congregation.*[7] For a more diverse list of faith-based organizations participating in disaster response, visit the University of Southern California's Center for Religion and Civic Culture.[8]

Regardless of whom you network with, the following will help you navigate the collaborative process. Having well-defined roles and responsibilities for each member of the network enhances organizational success and is one of the most critical factors in determining the success or failure of the network. The following are helpful steps for clarifying network member roles and responsibilities.[9]

- Identify the special resources that your church possesses (and potential gaps in knowledge, skills, resources and capacity).

- Decide upon action steps for leveraging resources (e.g., adapting resources or "pooling" together resources with other groups) and for addressing potential gaps. For example, a Meals on Wheels program could be leveraged to get food to volunteers or people who lost their homes.

- Make a written plan with other members about how your congregations will work together.

- Develop an understanding with your partners about what each other's specific role will be during disasters, based

Table 7.1

Examples of Christian Disaster Relief Organizations	
Mennonite Disaster Service	Episcopal Relief and Development
Lutheran Disaster Response	Covenant World Relief
Catholic Charities Office of Disaster Response	United Church of Christ National Disaster Ministries
Nazarene Disaster Response	United Methodist Committee on Relief (UMCOR)
Presbyterian Disaster Assistance	Friends Disaster Service
Christian Disaster Response	International Aid (Evangelical Christian)
Reformed Church World Service	World Relief
Anglican Relief and Development Fund	Church World Service
World Renew	Samaritan's Purse
Salvation Army	World Vision
Church of the Brethren Disaster Response	Church World Service
Southern Baptist Disaster Relief	Billy Graham Evangelistic Association Rapid Response Team

on the unique resources that it has (in coordination with others). For example, one church may have a counseling program and can provide emotional and spiritual care, while another may have a "chainsaw team" for clearing debris. Collaborating means combining your resources and operating as one team.

- Every six to twelve months, practice your disaster response plan as if a disaster has occurred. As you practice, make note of challenges and problems in the plan and decide how you will correct them.

- Work with your collaborators to modify the plan and address any challenges or problems that arise.

- Continue to meet to monitor and evaluate the plan and partnership.

Manage volunteers. Across almost every disaster we have responded to, we have heard disaster ministry leaders say something to the effect of, "The biggest blessing since the disaster has been the volunteers. And the biggest challenge since the disaster has been the volunteers." Volunteers can be a wonderful resource in the recovery process if you are prepared to manage them. Following are several recommendations to help you equip volunteers to serve effectively.

Recruit. Start by surveying or asking congregation members about their willingness to volunteer in case of disaster. People who have some direct experience with disasters are especially valuable volunteers. Look for congregation members with the following skills and character-

istics: prepared to be flexible and to respond to immediate survivor needs; able to adapt and improvise, to do the best with what is available; willing to be guided by leaders and survivors; sensitive to feelings of survivors; capable of working as part of a team, taking directions and overlooking irritations.

Train. Provide training for volunteers that covers topics including CPR, use of an Automated External Defibrillator (AED), first aid, listening, volunteering at evacuation shelters and assisting at immunization clinics. Training may be offered through organizations such as one of the Christian relief organizations mentioned above, local hospitals or clinics, and local health departments. You also need to take steps to be able to effectively manage volunteers from your church. The needs of volunteers typically fall into five main categories: housing, food, transportation, recreation and recognition/celebration. Consider the following:

- *Housing.* Where will volunteers stay? At a local church or some other facility? Does the location have adequate bathroom and shower facilities? Will the facility provide bedding, or do volunteers need to bring their own? Is there secure storage for volunteers' possessions?

- *Food.* Will food be provided? For which meals? Is the food adequate to keep volunteers well nourished as they serve in disaster relief? Are volunteers expected to pay anything to cover the cost of food?

- *Transportation.* How will volunteers get to and from the disaster area? How will they travel at the disaster site? Do road conditions make certain kinds of vehicles unusable? If driving, how many drivers are needed?

- *Recreation.* Recreation times while volunteers are serving are important for managing stress and helping volunteers to support one another. When will volunteers have time to relax together? Where can they go to rest and enjoy themselves?

- *Recognition/Celebration.* How can volunteers be recognized for their service in a way that is meaningful to them? Recognition can occur formally (e.g., a party or ceremony for volunteers after finishing their service) or informally (e.g., saying "thank you" to a volunteer for work he or she did).[10]

Orient. Finally, volunteers need to be oriented to the disaster situation they are about to serve in. They might have questions or concerns that should be addressed prior to starting their work. Orientation provides an opportunity to reduce their concerns and help them understand their role in the overall disaster response. Orientation usually occurs in three stages. The *first contact stage* (stage 1) is when volunteers initially express interest in helping with disaster recovery. This is a good time to provide an overview of the volunteer work and the types of skills required. The *predeparture stage* (stage 2) occurs as volunteers are getting ready to deploy for the disaster site. They should be given more detailed instructions about what to bring and what to expect when arriving at the site. The *arrival stage* (stage 3) is when volunteers first arrive at the disaster area and are likely to be a little anxious. Warmly welcoming them and providing an overview of the local community, logistical information, the work they will do, their living arrangements and safety information will help volunteers feel more at ease.[11]

Spiritual and emotional care. It is important to recognize that these individuals are not immune from burnout or distress. In fact, as we write elsewhere, "Because of their involvement with helping others who have been impacted, they are at risk. Thus, find ways to encourage self-care and healthy coping. This might include encouraging attendance at a self-care training or retreat, or time away from the disaster site. Another approach can be to bring resources, family and friends to the disaster site to minister to and support clergy or others carrying out this important work until they are ready for a break."[12] Many congregants, community members and responders would benefit from disaster spiritual and emotional care. Evaluate spiritual and emotional needs to decide whether congregational staff and leadership can provide the needed care and support. This evaluation will also aid in determining which congregants and community members are in need of care from a licensed mental health professional. It's likely that the need will be overwhelming, so in addition to pastoral care and counseling and peer support, determine other referral sources that are available in your community.[13]

Be aware of recovery equity in your area. Long-term recovery is where inequity in the community becomes most visible. People are not just at risk for the immediate impact of a disaster, but they are also at risk throughout the entire life cycle of the disaster, and most of all during the long-term recovery. It is during long-term recovery that differences in access to resources, the impact in government policy priorities and differences in rebuilding priorities are most visible. People who are medically vulnerable may find the services they depend upon are unavailable, such as the local pharmacy that has all their prescriptions, or public transportation so they can get to medical appointments. The elderly are more at risk to extreme temperatures, with high heat even contributing to the development of dementia in the elderly. In 1995 Chicago suffered a heat wave that led to 750 deaths in five days. The deaths were disproportionate to the poor and elderly, many of whom lived in older housing complexes where they had poor insulation, little or no air conditioning, and feared going out of the building due to the threat of being a victim of crime. These deaths were due to social factors more than the weather.

In just one more example, in 2011 Tuscaloosa-Birmingham was struck by an F5 tornado. It was one of 358 tornadoes that struck across twenty-eight states, the largest tornado outbreak in US history, and the second to hit Tuscaloosa in two weeks. Across six states, 348 people were killed. Shortly after this disaster we collaborated with Michael Parker and Gina McGaskill from the University of Alabama Medical School on a study focusing on the church and the elderly.[14] We found that 46 percent of the fatalities were among people over age fifty-five, and half of those among people over eighty. At the same time, 90 percent of the people over fifty-five were members of their local church. Unfortunately, none of those churches had any preparation program or communication plan to assist people during severe weather. In general, the poor, the fragile, the very old and very young, the people with the fewest resources and connections bear the brunt of any disaster. Therein lies an opportunity for the church, as well as one of the basic reasons we wrote this handbook. Disaster ministry is only partly about the church being prepared for an extreme event. It is even more so about the core ministry of the church to serve those in need. Disasters, as you will see, reveal the need for the church to serve the vulnerable.

Long periods without power or living in a shelter with inadequate heat or ventilation will put some people at grave risk. We previously mentioned how most communities will prioritize rebuilding large employers so people can get back to work, but what happens to the small business owner who lacks the financial reserves to wait for rebuilding, or the person who needs public housing and who has to wait a year before anything is available? Vulnerabilities compound themselves and create complex situations where a minority bear the majority of the community burden. Effective long-term recovery efforts need to be aware of these needs so that those with extreme needs are cared for.

But how exactly do you do that? You need to know who these people are. When you do your assessment of the vulnerable in and around your church, remember vulnerability is not temporary. The way the vulnerability shows itself shifts as the disaster progresses from immediate relief to long-term recovery. The person who needs help with transportation to evacuate from the path of a tornado may later need help getting out to buy food and medicine or getting to medical appointments or out to apply for assistance. The vulnerability did not end with the immediate crisis; its form just shifted with the changing circumstances.

Form a long-term unmet-needs committee. After a disaster strikes, most of the funding, aid and resources all pour in during the immediate aftermath of the catastrophe. What many people don't realize is that some disasters can result in years of recovery efforts before a community is back on its feet. Overall, in most disasters, the need is greater than the resources available, especially as the recovery process drags on. This is especially true for those who are most vulnerable, whose recovery process often takes the longest. As a result, it is common for coalitions of members from the faith community, nonprofit agencies, government programs and business and individual donors to come together to step into this gap and to form a long-term unmet-needs committee or long-term recovery committee. Together, they work to identify those still in need.[15]

Sometimes people get identified by members of the committee, local churches or other community members or organizations. In most cases, though, people who are referred to the committee have sought FEMA assistance but their needs go beyond what FEMA and the state can provide. The committee meets and reviews and makes decisions on expenditures and use of volunteer resources on a case-by-case basis. During their meetings needs are discussed and attempts are made to match resources accordingly. In most cases, they work to match eligible individuals and families with donated materials, assistance by volunteer work crews and/or contracted skilled labor. In most cases, the committee will provide a case manger to work with each family in assessing damage, formulating a recovery plan and procuring cost estimates. It is important to note, however, that these committees expect families to use all private insurance and federal disaster grants and loans before applying for assistance.[16]

Assist with case management. Disaster case management, according to the Federal Emergency Management Agency, is a time-limited process that involves connecting a case manager and a disaster survivor to develop and carry out a disaster recovery plan. This approach provides the survivor with a single point of contact to facilitate access to a broad range of resources. The process involves an assessment of the survivor's verified disaster-caused unmet needs. It also includes development of a goal-oriented plan that outlines the steps necessary to achieve recovery, organization and coordination of information on available resources that match the disaster-caused unmet needs. Case management also allows for a survivor's progress toward recovery plan goals and, when necessary, client advocacy.[17]

Sometimes a large Christian disaster relief organization (e.g., UMCOR or Church World Service) will deploy to a community significantly affected by a disaster and help organize and engage local churches in providing case management services. Other times, local churches may decide to collaborate with local, state or federal emergency management agencies to help provide case management services. If perhaps there are serious losses, but not large enough for other organizations to warrant coming in and helping establish case management services, local churches may find themselves running such services in connection with a local long-term unmet-needs committee.

Help with reconstruction. After a disaster, repairs or rebuilding may be necessary for your grounds and building. Perform safety checks to figure out which parts of the building can be used, and make a plan to repair damaged parts. This is an opportunity to serve your congregants and community. You could establish a team of volunteers with experience in construction to supervise clearing out, repairing or rebuilding homes for congregants or church members whose homes have been damaged. Or you can work with another organization that focuses on such services (e.g., Mennonite Disaster Services, Samaritan's Purse).

Manage donations. We recognize the financial needs following a disaster can feel overwhelming. In a disaster situation, financial resources function as a critical asset that can become overwhelming, and even mismanaged, if a church is unprepared for the unique financial challenges and opportunities inherent in a disaster. Write down every action taken during the response and all donations. This will provide a record of not just donations, but also time and effort. This will help track the work you have done, assist with transparency and help with taxes. You may also need to make a record of damage for insurance purposes and track expenses connected to the event. Keep all original notes and records. The following are additional recommendations intended to help your church make appropriate financial preparations for disasters and to know what steps to take once a disaster occurs.

Appoint a reliable church member (or team of church members) to have access to savings accounts during a disaster. Ensure that bank documents are kept in a secure location where they will not get damaged by disaster conditions. At the same time, these documents need to be accessible should they be required for financial transactions. You want to make sure that you carefully document the amount and type of funds/goods collected and distributed. Be aware of local fundraising regulations to ensure all legal requirements are met while raising financial and material support. Since electricity may be unavailable after a disaster, plan to keep physical records (e.g., accounting ledgers) if computers do not work.

Keep emergency cash on hand, in case funds are unavailable electronically. Discuss plans with your church financial team and bank personnel to ensure staff will receive salaries in the midst of disaster conditions. Appoint a church member (or team) to be responsible for purchasing supplies for the church following a disaster. Purchase basic emergency supplies in advance, since these may be unavailable to buy in the aftermath of a disaster. Keep some cash in a safe but accessible location for postdisaster purchases.

Appoint a church member or team to manage donations of money and goods. Find a secure, dry location where goods may be kept. Ensure food items are properly stored to prevent spoiling. Discuss with church leaders whether donations should be kept for church ministry use or contributed to a denomination, church network or other organization. Prior to a disaster, decide who will have authority to make financial decisions for the church in an emergency situation. Consider appointing a financial leadership team to manage the tasks described above.

Raising money for disaster relief is a very important task, but before requesting donations, keep the following points in mind. Support effective local disaster organizations, instead of creating another disaster ministry, when possible. Determine whether nonprofit or service organizations are already doing the work you want to support. Consider how the money is used—that is, what percentage actually goes to relief efforts, and what percentage is used for administrative costs. Partner with other local churches or organizations to plan how funds or other donated materials will be used; this will help to ensure that resources are spread evenly across all areas of need. Focus fundraising efforts on specific needs—exact quantities and specific time frames—in order to avoid wasting time, money and space on superfluous goods. Plan how to politely decline goods that are not needed; clearly communicate what is needed and how it will be used; and generally avoid accepting gift cards, particularly from international donors, as they may not be accepted if purchased abroad.[18]

Observe disaster anniversaries. Many things will trigger congregants and community members to recall the disaster. The anniversary in particular will bring up memories and feelings about the event, but other occasions may do this as well—holidays along with events that don't seem to have any link to the incident. This is a reminder that recovery may take longer than you expect. Leaders need to take note of their own reactions along with those of congregants and community members on such occasions and be supportive when needed. Consider holding pertinent memorial services or other events such as a community-wide prayer or worship service.

Evaluate. Assessing recovery efforts will help preparation for the next disaster. We recommend several methods to do this. Perform brief interviews with emergency responders, congregation members and staff, and also consider using focus groups to get honest responses to recovery efforts. The following are examples of questions to ask.[19]

- Which congregational interventions proved most successful and why?

- Which assessment and referral strategies were the most successful and why?

- What were the most positive aspects of providing disaster spiritual and emotional care and why?

- Which recovery strategies would you change and why?

- Do other professionals need to be tapped to help with future crises?

- What additional training is necessary to

enable the congregation and the community at large to better prepare for future disasters?

- What additional equipment or supplies are needed to support recovery efforts?

- What other planning actions will facilitate future recovery efforts?

Helping Other Churches and Communities (Beyond Your Community)

One of the most common questions we get from churches after a disaster is, "How can we help from a distance?" Disasters can bring out the best in us. Congregations often want to help after disasters, and communities affected by disasters need people to help. However, sometimes our good intentions can actually cause more harm than good if we are not careful. In this section we help you learn how you can help other churches and communities (outside of your community) affected by disasters. More specifically, we discuss ways your church can help without causing unintentional harm.

Keep your focus on the survivors' needs. As I (Jamie) wrote in a *Christianity Today* article, I have a colleague who has done a lot of research following large oil spills.[20] He shared with me that after the Exxon Valdez, many of the local communities were overwhelmed by the support that was lent from all over the world. Though most of the support was positive, some people sent goods that actually placed more burdens on the community. For example, people from all over sent literally tons of clothes, which the communities had to sort and distribute appropriately. Up to this

point it sounds helpful. However, they actually had people send barrels and barrels of summer clothes and even swimsuits, which are not very helpful in the wintery climate off the Alaskan coast. In the end, these communities were stuck with over a $200,000 bill just to get rid of the clothes they could not use.

Educate yourself about survivors' needs. Survivors can experience a wide range of needs following a disaster, including physical, emotional and spiritual needs, so various types of support can be helpful. But we should also consider the actual amount of need. Referring back to my colleague's story about Alaska, it is possible to give too much. Keep in mind that aid happens where need meets resources. Do your best to find out, from your own contacts or local or national organizations, exactly what types of aid and volunteers are necessary. Knowledge is power. Affiliating with nonprofit organizations like Salvation Army or Red Cross that have established relationships and resources is another way you can ensure you are more likely to help and not hurt. Perhaps you are not sure which organization to volunteer with or to give to. If a good Internet search is not enough, consider reaching out to a Volunteer Reception Center that has been established by relief organizations in the community affected that can help connect you to volunteer opportunities or connect your resources more easily with people in need.

Understand your motivation for wanting to help. When we help we need to keep our focus on the disaster survivors themselves and make sure we are helping for the right reason. As I (Jamie) wrote elsewhere,

"Giving a gift can make us feel good and make a huge positive impact on the life of a survivor—but only if it is the right gift at the right time, for the right reasons. After Hurricane Katrina I learned of a church that really wanted to donate food to disaster survivors. They rented a semi-truck and took about $60,000 worth of frozen meals to the coast. Despite groups on the ground trying to discourage this approach, church leaders had made up their mind that this was how they were going to help. On arrival, they realized there was no electricity to cook the meals or to refrigerate it. The meals went to waste and actually rotted alongside the road."[21] Prior to helping, try to understand your own reasons for helping as well as what the actual needs are. Some people desire to help in order to be in "the action" and to see what is happening. Others appreciate the community bonds that result from such work. Others want to be recognized as doing good. Others feel called by faith to help in whatever way necessary. I want to encourage you and your church to be the latter.

Volunteer, but do not be an SUV. I also want to urge you not to self-deploy. Spontaneous unaffiliated volunteers (SUV) can bring chaos to a disaster recovery site and even hinder those authorized to offer special aid. I relate to wanting to pick up and "parachute" down into a location where a disaster has occurred. As a result of studying numerous disasters, however, I have found that doing so frequently causes a great deal of stress to those in need of help. Rather than hopping in the car and driving off to the site, restrain yourself until volunteer opportunities have been

clearly identified. Further, if you do go and volunteer, prepare to be self-sufficient. Communities in the midst of recovery need to concentrate resources on survivors and not on meeting your needs, such as helping you locate appropriate shelter. Those of you reading who want to go help should also remember that it can be good to be patient. Traumatized communities will need aid for months or even years afterward. Actually, many places receive a flood of volunteers immediately after a disaster (which is good), but then aid peters out as people forget about the disaster in the time that follows, a time when help is still much needed. Consider waiting and participating in the long-term recovery process, or working with an established group like Samaritan's Purse. Or if you have a specialized skill or just an overwhelming sense of calling to go early on, consider going multiple times so that long-term needs are also met.

Give. Though many of us want to go and volunteer or donate items, one of the most effective ways you can help is to raise donations to support disaster survivors. Overall, our research has found that one of the most effective ways to help after a disaster is to make financial contributions to recognized disaster relief organizations. Financial contributions make sure that the right assistance is available at the right time. Demands on the ground adjust quickly, and money can be shifted from a meal to supplies. I know we often like to give gifts and items, and this desire makes sense. We feel more personally connected this way—sometimes we even imagine someone in particular getting the gift we have sent. Following the 2012 Sandy Hook Elementary School tragedy in Newtown, Connecticut, people from all over the world donated toys and teddy bears. These gifts helped a number of families, but they eventually came to overwhelm the community. They were forced to issue a statement saying "please stop sending gifts." Financial contributions, on the other hand, allow those on the scene with the greatest amount of knowledge to decide how best to apply the gifts at the time. So how do you decide on what organization(s) you should give to? The first place to start is to donate to a trusted organization that shares your values.[22]

Conclusion

Recovery does not happen overnight. Long-term disaster recovery takes time, sometimes years. Thus, it is important that your church keep an extended view in mind when developing your disaster ministry. Though there will be some similarities, the needs of your church and community will inevitably be different in the recovery phase than the needs present in the response phase. This means you may need a different focus, skills and approach

to carrying out your disaster ministry over the long haul. Working with others is one of the best strategies we have found to assist in recovery. Don't go alone—reach out and work with others. It will help you be able to prolong your ministry. Working together also allows each church and organization to leverage their strengths and pool them together.

Discussion Questions

1. If you needed to rebuild and were without a church building for some length of time, where would you find the resources to continue? Who would be your community partners to help you recover?

2. What are your emotional and spiritual care resources? Do you have mental health people among your members? Do you have a counseling program at the church? Discuss how they can be leveraged for disaster ministry.

3. Do you have other programs that include training volunteers? What have they taught you about the challenges of a training program? How do you build on the experience of others as you design this ministry?

chapter eight

Providing Basic Disaster Spiritual and Emotional Care

Several months after the 3/11 disaster struck Japan, we visited some of the areas most heavily affected by the earthquake, tsunami and nuclear plant meltdown. I (Jamie) vividly remember viewing a community that had all but been wiped away from on top of a giant seawall as I stood side by side with David and the rest of our team. The seawall had been built years ago to protect the community below from tsunamis. The massive concrete structure consisted of two crisscrossing intersecting walls in order to provide two layers of protection, in what looked like a giant concrete X. After it was first built, people came from all over the country to see this incredible engineering feat.

Though the seawall was still standing, the same could not be said for the community below. The tsunami waves were so enormous they crashed right over the wall. The waves swept through the town below and ran up against a mountainside on the other side of the town. The waters then slid back down the mountains and tore back through the community until they crashed back into the seawall. So there we stood, on top of what was previously thought to be an impenetrable wall. Most of the town's buildings had been literally swept away. Many of the structures that were still standing were gutted out. We also saw heavy machinery, like industrial backhoes and bulldozers, pushing and scooping debris into giant mounds of rubble.

After making our way down what seemed like an endless staircase from the seawall, we drove out to a large shelter where many of the people who had lived in the community now lived. We went with a team of church leaders to assess the mental health challenges facing the disaster survivors. One of the pastors with us shared a quote from a survivor he had recently visited. She said, "Every time you come, a piece of rubble is removed from my heart." Progress had been made in clearing the physical damage that remained in the wake of this catastrophe. However, stories like this bring to light that disasters can leave behind real emotional, cognitive and spiritual "rubble" among the inner lives of many who are affected. We see in these stories that resilience and hope endure and that healing is possible.

Over the next several years we worked closely with the support of World Relief to collaborate with the Japanese Evangelical Association, CRASH Japan, Salvation Army, Covenant World Relief, Tokyo Christian University and a host of local churches and church networks. In addition to helping address the physical needs of survivors, such as helping with rebuilding homes and providing meals, the churches also ministered to the internal wounds of survivors. One of the common ways churches helped was by providing basic social support. Volunteers spent countless hours listening to the stories of survivors as they helped address other needs. Other survivors helped identify and address unmet and urgent needs. Some volunteers had opportunities to pray and offer encouragement. Overall, several of the survivors we talked to that had been helped shared how deeply people had ministered to them by providing a shoulder to cry on and a listening ear.

The churches also worked with local authorities to visit the shelters to serve small meals and tea and lead worship. Many of the survivors tended to isolate themselves from others, especially the men. The churches intentionally worked at creating events and opportunities that would bring people together. For example, while we were there, the churches helped arrange for a well-known local musician to come and perform. It was particularly moving when one of the church leaders invited an elderly man sitting by himself in the back to come up and help lead the group in shared childhood songs. You could see new life breathed not only into this man's face, but into the faces of everyone there. For the first time in our visit at the shelters, we saw smiles and people coming together, laughing and talking. The volunteers from the church then served tea and led the group in several hymns. The volunteers were able to help provide hope and meaning to what the survivors had gone through.

Organizations like CRASH Japan and the Salvation Army helped train disaster chaplains who provided disaster spiritual and emotional care to those in need. Yet they also were trained in more advanced helping skills. For example, they had been trained in how to recognize and address spiritual struggles common after a disaster. The chaplains were also ready to address common crises. They knew what types of spiritual and emotional problems to look for that might warrant a referral.

The Salvation Army also helped build a food court in a community that had all been swept away. This brought businesses, and more importantly, people back together. People now had a place they could go and visit and support one another. This is an example of a community approach to providing disaster spiritual and emotional care. In fact, the Salvation Army received an award for their community-focused efforts from the Japanese government—a rare event for a Christian organization to receive this honor.

In addition to providing disaster spiritual and emotional care for survivors, these groups also sought to care for the caregivers. One of the major challenges the churches noticed was that many people helping with the relief efforts were burning out. We worked with our partners and local churches to provide several trainings on preventing burnout among clergy, volunteers and disaster relief staff. Some of the groups also regularly set aside time for volunteers to share their stories from the day and to provide support for one another. Other groups led brief retreats for staff to get away, even if just for a short time, for a period of reflection and renewal. Overall, these are just a few of the ways that disaster spiritual and emotional care were provided.

Purpose

The purpose of this chapter is to introduce you to basic disaster spiritual and emotional care helping strategies. We have devoted an entire chapter to this subject because we believe it cuts across all disaster ministry activities. This chapter focuses on delivering supportive care while avoiding the pitfalls of well-intentioned but unhelpful advice giving. It will help you recognize what is (and is not) healthy support. In this chapter we also offer recommendations for supporting the emotional and spiritual needs of children affected by disasters. We will cover guidelines for referring survivors for additional mental health care, as well as strategies for recognizing and preventing burnout and secondary trauma.

Be Aware of Common Stress Reactions to Disasters

Catastrophic events can be traumatic, and people may be affected in extensive and varied ways. Most people are able to bounce back and have mild or passing psychological struggles. But how much "normal stress reaction" qualifies as too much? Many of the reactions listed in table 8.1 are experienced by those who have survived disaster and have limited long-term consequences. They become problematic when they persist over time and when they start to interfere with everyday life. Further, when a number of reactions are experienced simultaneously and intensely, people are more likely to become impaired. Table 8.1 illustrates the range and type of reactions and provides an overview of common stress reactions to disasters. Though everyone reacts differently to a disaster, these are some common reactions you might observe and should watch for.[1]

Listen for Common Spiritual Struggles

Our faith influences how we make sense of the world. Survivors may seek comfort that comes from their beliefs. As we write elsewhere, "Spiritual beliefs will assist some survivors with coping and resilience. At the same time, disasters can also lead to spiritual struggles as survivors attempt to make meaning of their disaster experience. Research has shown that persistent spiritual struggles are linked to more negative emotional and physical health symptoms among disaster survivors." Many people seek out clergy after disasters for help working through spiritual struggles. Examples of common spiritual struggles include:

- Spiritual meaning—"Why would a good God let such a bad thing happen? I just can't understand."

Table 8.1[2]

Common Psychological and Emotional Reactions	
Sadness, grief, depression, moodiness	Denial
Anxiety and fear	Distressing dreams
Guilt or "survivor guilt"	Feeling overwhelmed, hopeless
Worry about safety of self and others	Feeling isolated, lost or abandoned
Anger	Irritability and restlessness
Common Cognitive Reactions	
Memory problems, especially short-term memory	Poor concentration
Disorientation	Confusion
Slowness of thinking and comprehension	Difficulty calculating, setting priorities, making decisions
Limited attention span	Loss of objectivity
Inability to stop thinking about the disaster	Blaming
Common Behavioral Reactions	
Change in activity	Decreased efficiency and effectiveness
Difficulty communicating	Outbursts of anger, frequent arguments
Inability to rest or "let down"	Change in eating habits
Change in sleeping patterns	Change in patterns of intimacy
Change in job performance	Periods of crying
Increased use of alcohol, tobacco, drugs	Social withdrawal, silence
Vigilance about safety or environment	Avoidance of activities or places that trigger memories
Common Physical Reactions	
Increased heartbeat, respiration	Feeling uncoordinated
Increased blood pressure	Headaches
Upset stomach, nausea, diarrhea	Soreness in muscles
Change in appetite, weight loss or gain	Lower back pain
Feeling a "lump in the throat"	Exaggerated startle reaction
Fatigue	Menstrual cycle changes
Change in sexual desire	Decreased resistance to infection
Common Spiritual Reactions	
Questions about faith	Questioning God
Anger at God	Realization of mortality
Withdrawal from faith and religion	Concern about hereafter
Questions about good and evil	Redefining moral values and intangible priorities
Promising, bargaining with and challenging God	Search for meaning
Questions about forgiveness	Belief of being punished for sins

- Spiritual control and responsibility—"Did I do something to cause God to punish me?" "Why would God allow this to happen?"

- Spiritual disconnection and isolation—"Has God abandoned me?"

- Religious strain—"I feel like God is so far away right now."[3]

Adopt a "Strength" Focus for Helping

Focusing on the survivor's strengths is essential for bolstering their coping and helping them through the crisis stage. In times of crisis it is important for helpers, both lay volunteers and professionals, to recognize that the counsel people need most is that which supports their strengths and ability to cope, thus helping them through the crisis. Almost anything can be considered a strength, including taking steps to protect yourself, such as removing yourself from a threat; making necessary decisions even when feeling overwhelmed; recognizing a need for assistance; and maintaining hope, courage or a sense of humor. You can find a person's strengths by listening to their story. Thus, the use of basic listening skills to solicit the survivor's experience and learn how they cope and survive is essential.

Utilize Basic Listening Skills

To be effective in helping survivors, we need to be able to be present in the here and now, and to grasp both verbal and nonverbal messages being communicated by those we are helping. Active listening means responding in a way that shows you are paying attention and that you understood what you heard. It is based on the assumption that listening is just the start; you must also *show* that you are listening, hence the term "active listening."

Here are some listening skills to help you improve your helping effectiveness:

- Acknowledge the difficulty of the situation.

- To the extent possible, be there through the difficulties.

- Be willing to listen to the hard parts of the story.

- Relate to the survivor through his or her worldview.

- Help the survivor manage anxiety and other emotions.

- Notice and remark about the strengths and changes that come from the struggle.

- Do not offer platitudes.

- Listen for survivors who show evidence of being suicidal, psychotic or unable to care for themselves. They should be referred to mental health professionals for support.[4]

Practice the Ministry of Presence

In almost every major disaster we have responded to, we have heard clergy and church leaders report feeling overwhelmed by not knowing how to help. Yet many go on to discuss that they learned the power of practicing the ministry of presence, which is our ability to create a sacred space for us to bond and build a healthy relationship with others. Presence is what takes place as you prepare to talk with someone. It is about getting yourself ready, orienting yourself to what is going on in the surroundings and

Listen!

becoming aware of the person you plan to assist. Before you approach a person for the first time or meet with them for a follow-up, take a few moments and observe what is going on around you and with the person. For example, if you are entering a temporary shelter, you might look to see who needs assistance, what people are doing and what risks people are currently exposed to (if any). In establishing presence you start by putting aside other concerns and paying attention to the setting and the person you are going to speak with.[5]

You invite the person to speak with you. Be prepared for people to decline this offer. You make them aware that you are available, but it is entirely their choice if they speak with you. If a person does speak with you, you focus on letting them tell their story. Remember, this is about being with a person and showing interest, concern and caring; it is not about "fixing" something or someone. Remember that a story may unfold a bit at a time over time. Even if you have spoken with a person before, there is likely to be more to their story. Be prepared to keep the person's information confidential. This is not just a policy; it is part of respect for the person and needs to be something that is clear in your own mind before you start. Being present means focusing on demonstrating compassion and respect. We know from research on the helping process that the relationship between the helper and the person receiving help is the most important factor in determining success. Said differently, the helper as a person is a key part of the effectiveness of the helping. Another way you can practice the ministry

of presence is through prayer. You can pray internally to ask for God's guidance, pray to enter the helping process, and pray on behalf of the person you are helping. Or you might consider praying with the person out loud. However, before doing so, it is good to ask the survivor if it is okay to pray for them. Another approach is to ask the person if they would like to offer a prayer. If the person says no or hesitates, do not force the prayer.

If the person is welcoming of prayer, you might also use prayer as a way to model communicating with God to the person you are assisting. It shows the person you are praying for how you perceive God and models relating to God as a resource. Incorporate your message to the person into prayer. In your prayer, saying what the trauma means to the person and offering that to God conveys that God understands at a very personal level. In prayer and in other communications, it is important to avoid making false assurances (e.g., "God will protect you from being overwhelmed") or offering simple solutions (e.g., "God will fix everything"). At the same time, perhaps you feel at a loss for words; this too is okay. Communicating that you aren't sure what to say but that God is still present and hears even what we cannot express verbally can be just as powerful as the well-worded prayer. These approaches communicate to a person that you and/or God understand their situation.

This brief introduction only serves as a reminder to use prayer in your disaster ministry, and a suggestion on how to go about it. We encourage further reading on this important topic.[6]

Assess Spiritual/Pastoral Strengths and Resources

Assess what spiritual and religious resources are already available to people. Listen to what immediate needs they may have for spiritual support. Consider using Scripture and prayer—some people may feel comforted by Scripture passages being read. Others may want to offer specific prayers. Some will be comforted simply by the assurance that you will pray for them. Let them take the lead in suggesting what they find to be comforting and helpful. Here are four examples of questions that can be used to explore their spiritual resources:

1. Is there a faith community that they have a relationship with?

2. Are there clergy they might want to have contacted?

3. In difficult times, do they find it helpful to pray?

4. Would they want you to offer a prayer with them?

General Guidelines for How to (and How Not to) Respond to Disaster Spiritual Issues

Church World Service recommends strategies for responding to disaster spiritual issues that may surface in circumstances following crises:[8]

- Use reflective listening and active listening techniques covered above when working with victims/survivors.

- Be honest, with compassion, and do not assume you know what they will say or believe.

- If you do not feel comfortable discussing spiritual/religious issues, listen quietly and refer them to someone who can help them appropriately.

- Do not try to explain or give answers to spiritual questions.

- Do not argue with their beliefs or try to persuade them to believe as you do.

- Do not respond with platitudes or clichés, such as, "It will be okay," "It is God's will," "They are in a better place."

- Let them tell you what their religious/spiritual beliefs are. Do not assume anything.

- Help them use their spiritual/religious beliefs to cope.

- They may need reassurance that it is "normal" to ask questions about God and/or their religious beliefs.

- Allow expressions of anger toward God or others, and assess whether they are a danger to themselves or others.

- Affirm their search for spiritual/faith-based answers. Do not impose your thoughts or beliefs on them.

- Affirm the wrongness and/or injustice of what has happened, especially if the trauma was caused by people.

- Encourage them to turn to religious or spiritual writings within their culture that bring them comfort and help them in their search for meaning or spiritual answers.

- Emphasize that everyone has to find their own answers and way of understanding in traumatic events.

When providing support, there are certain

104 DISASTER MINISTRY HANDBOOK

104 DISASTER MINISTRY HANDBOOK

phrases to avoid saying. On the surface, these phrases may be meant to comfort the survivors, but they can be misinterpreted. Basic statements to avoid include the following:

- "I understand." In most situations we cannot understand unless we have had the same experience.

- "Don't feel bad." The survivor has a right to feel bad and will need time to feel differently.

- "You're strong" or "You'll get through this." Many survivors do not feel strong and question if they will recover from the loss.

- "Don't cry." It is okay to cry.

- "It's God's will." With a person you do not know, giving religious meaning to an event may insult or anger the person.

- "It could be worse," "At least you still have . . .," or "Everything will be okay." It is up to the individual to decide whether things could be worse or if everything can be okay.[9]

Rather than provide comfort, these types of responses could elicit a strong negative response or distance the survivor from you. It is okay to apologize if the survivor reacts negatively to something that was said.[10]

Help Stabilize the Situation and Make Sure the Person Is Safe

A more traditional counseling approach emphasizes exploring, examining and questioning, which are generally not helpful in a crisis and best set aside till the crisis stage is over. A strength focus emphasizes nourishing success and ability, un-

leashing the survivor's ability and pointing out positive, even strong, characteristics that the survivor can utilize to get through the crisis. Keep the focus more practical and immediate (i.e., get through the crisis). The goal here is to help the person hold themselves together through the initial crisis until they have the coping and capacity to explore the loss in more depth. The ideal outcome is that you would help survivors feel safe, calm, connected to others, empowered and hopeful. To help stabilize the person, you remind the person that there are people ready to help. Listen for what the survivor wants and then help them connect to their resources and strengths to get there.

Following are some examples of what to do to help stabilize the situation and to help make sure they are safe. Help the survivor meet basic needs for food and shelter and obtain emergency medical attention. Provide repeated, simple and accurate information on how to obtain these while emphasizing safety. Listen closely to those who wish to share their stories and emotions and remember there is no wrong or right way to feel in the aftermath of a disaster. With that in mind, also be careful not to try and force others to share before they are ready. Focus on being friendly and compassionate even if people are being difficult. Provide accurate information about the disaster or trauma and the relief efforts underway to the best of your knowledge. If you don't know an answer to their question, do your best to find out, but don't make an error in responding to questions that you don't actually know the answers to. This will help people to understand the situation. Whenever possible help people contact and connect with friends or loved ones and work to keep families together. For example, if you are working in a shelter, help keep parents with their children; separating them from one another can cause significant amounts of anxiety and fear, especially for the children.

Remember that helping the survivor locate a family member is just as important (if not more important) to their spiritual and emotional well-being as processing their emotions during the early phase of responding. In fact, research has shown that trying to delve too deeply too quickly after a disaster into a survivor's emotions and thoughts can actually cause harm.[11] In most cases, this type of help is more appropriate several weeks or a few months after the disaster has occurred. In the early phase after a disaster, your focus should be on making sure that the person has resources to care for their basic needs. Do they have access to food and water, shelter, and so on? Also, research has shown an increase in domestic violence, anger and the like after disasters.[12] Thus, you also want to check in to make sure the person is safe in their current living arrangements. After Hurricane Katrina there were many reports of criminal and sexual assaults on survivors staying in the Superdome shelter. Check in with the person you are helping to make sure that their larger environment is safe.[13]

Helping Children Cope with Disasters

Shortly after 9/11, parents of a five-year-old boy mentioned to me that they'd noticed their son reenacting the collapse of the Twin Towers with his Legos. Absorbed by the news coverage themselves, they hadn't realized until that moment just how much information their young son had taken in. Whether children experience trauma or acts of violence personally, have seen an event on television or heard it discussed by peers or adults, they may become frightened, confused and insecure. For this reason, it's important to be informed about how to provide disaster spiritual and emotional care to children—to recognize the signs of reactions to stress and to learn how to best help children cope. Next we discuss how to recognize signs of trauma among children, how to meet their spiritual needs and steps for reassuring them.

Recognize the signs. For many children, reactions to disasters are simply normal reactions to abnormal events. But what sorts of reactions may point to the need for further help? Signs to watch for may include major changes in sleep patterns (including trouble falling asleep, frequent nightmares or sleeping too much); shifts in temperament (for instance, a quiet child may act out or become easily agitated or irritable, while a gregarious child may withdraw socially); and even jumpiness, increased anxiety or changes in play. Of course, the risk of enduring psychological distress increases given the circumstances. Children at a higher risk include those who experience direct exposure to the disaster—including being evacuated, observing the injury or death of others, experiencing injury themselves, or fearing for their lives. Those grieving the loss of family or friends, those still experiencing ongoing stressors such as temporary living situations or losing touch with friends, teachers and social networks are also at a greater risk for experiencing long-term consequences.[14]

About a year after Hurricane Katrina hit the Gulf Coast, I remember meeting with a group of local community leaders and health care professionals who were very concerned about the increase of bipolar disorder diagnoses among children in their community. As they talked about the symptoms these children were exhibiting, I began writing them up on the chalkboard for all to see. It soon became clear that what they were seeing were the snowball effects of reactions to ongoing trauma. This experience made me realize just how important it is for parents, caregivers and entire communities to understand the impact and effects that trauma can have, to be able to recognize the warning signs of reactions to stress for what they are and to remain aware, since these responses aren't always immediate.[15]

Meeting a child's spiritual needs. Providing spiritual support to children after a disaster can be as simple as remaining open to questions, thoughts or feelings children might share about faith—and understanding that it is common for children, especially those directly affected by disasters, to experience spiritual struggles, including doubts about the nature of God. Taking a developmental approach to addressing spiritual issues can be as simple as asking the question back to the child in order to understand how the child is interpreting or making meaning of an event. For example, when asked, "Why would God allow this to happen?" your reply might be, "What are your thoughts?" This

helps you assess where the child is developmentally before responding. Remember that you don't have to have all the answers. In my experience, it's better to admit that you don't know than to respond thoughtlessly. It is perfectly fine to tell a child you'll think about their question, or pray about it, and then to consult with a pastor, church leader or counselor first before answering any question you aren't prepared to answer on your own.

Another useful approach is to share encouraging stories, songs, Scripture or prayers. Discuss the proactive and redemptive things that also sometimes occur during or following traumatic events. The Old Testament stories of God's care for Joseph, Moses and the children of Abraham can provide reassurance, but don't be afraid to tell present-day stories as well. A colleague and I (Jamie) did a study after the San Francisco earthquake about how children perceive God. One child who had been on the bridge during the earthquake drew a picture showing a tangled bridge with the arms of God wrapped around his family.[16] It was a beautiful illustration of how even in the midst of tragedy, God isn't somewhere else; he's right there with us. Similarly, it's important to maintain spiritual routines or practices in the home and community. Older children may benefit from journaling about spiritual challenges arising from the event, whereas younger children might draw pictures as a way of expressing their spiritual concerns.[17]

Steps for reassuring children. The first step you can take to help a child cope emotionally with trauma involves providing as safe and calm an environment as possible, remembering that children's reactions are often influenced by the behavior, thoughts and feelings of the adults around them. Never treat a child like a peer, expecting them to process your emotions as well as their own. Instead, seek pastoral help or the wise counsel of friends or professional counselors so that you can appropriately support the children in your care. Help those around the child reestablish their daily routine for work, school, play, meals and rest as soon as possible (consistency is an important source of security for children). You might also recommend that caregivers involve children by giving them specific chores, allowing them to feel they are helping to restore family and community life. Be sure to praise and recognize responsible behavior.

The second step involves encouraging (but not pushing) children and adolescents to share their thoughts and feelings about the incident. If a child has difficulty expressing feelings, coloring, drawing a picture, telling a story or playing with stuffed animals together can be great conversation starters. It's also important to reinforce good memories by making time to do something positive together. This can be as simple as chatting while playing catch outside together. As conversations come up, take the opportunity to clarify misunderstandings about risk and danger by listening to children's concerns and answering their questions. Maintain a sense of calm by validating their fears and perceptions with a discussion of concrete plans for safety—at home, church and school, when appropriate. Listen to what the child is saying. If a young child is asking questions about the event, answer them directly and clearly, without the longer explanations required for an adult or older child. It is best to give a straightforward, honest response. Do not, for example, say to a young child that a deceased person has gone on a long trip or is merely sleeping, since this may cause more anxiety about people leaving or falling asleep. Some children are comforted by knowing more or less information than others; decide what level of information your particular child needs. Remember not to dismiss a child's feelings. Reactions to a disaster can vary from anger to sorrow to anything in between. It's important to affirm whatever the child is feeling. Make sure they know it's okay to cry, and don't say things like, "Don't be sad" or "You just have to pull yourself together." Remember that if a child uncharacteristically lashes out, getting to the root of what's really bothering them can help.

The third step is to monitor and limit exposure to the media. News coverage related to a disaster may elicit fear and confusion and arouse anxiety in children. This is especially the case for horrific acts of violence where there have been a number of fatalities. Especially for younger children, seeing images of the incident over and over may lead them to think the event is happening again and again. If children are watching television or accessing the internet where images or stories about the disaster are available, parents should be present to foster communication and offer explanations. You might also encourage parents of older children to monitor their child's use of social networking sites as these may be sources for further exposure to incorrect information and angry, fear-inducing comments.

The fourth step is to encourage caregivers to simply spend extra time with their children, especially at bedtime. If you've tried these recommendations and have helped caregivers to create a reassuring environment by following the steps above, but the child continues to exhibit stress, you may need to refer. If the reactions worsen over time, or these reactions begin to cause interference with daily behavior at school, church or home, it may be appropriate to talk to a professional. You can get professional help from the child's primary care physician, a mental health provider specializing in children's needs or a member of the clergy. Further, you can follow the steps below for more recommendations on when and how to refer.[18]

When and How to Refer

It is important to remember that some disaster survivors may need additional follow-up services from a licensed mental health professional. Similarly, some relief workers and volunteers may need additional assistance after particularly traumatic events. Here we discuss when and how to refer others for mental health care from a licensed professional (e.g., counselor, marriage and family therapist, pastoral counselor, psychologist, psychiatrist, social worker).

When to refer. The need for more serious help is indicated by more severe symptoms—ones that go on for more than a few days or ones that appear much later.

Some people's emotional reactions become unpredictable or extreme, and their behavior becomes impulsive or risky in a manner unlike them, or they turn to self-medication with drugs or alcohol. Signs for concern include the following:[19]

- Disorientation or confusion and difficulty communicating thoughts
- Difficulty remembering instructions
- Difficulty maintaining balance
- Becoming easily frustrated and being uncharacteristically argumentative
- Inability to engage in problem solving and difficulty making decisions
- Unnecessary risk taking
- Tremors, headaches and nausea
- Unusual clumsiness
- Tunnel vision and muffled hearing
- Colds or flu-like symptoms
- Limited attention span and difficulty concentrating
- Loss of objectivity
- Inability to relax
- Increased use of drugs or alcohol

Do not be afraid to acknowledge that you don't know how to solve a problem or that further care is needed. Just offer to help the person find someone who might know or has specific training. As you refer disaster victims to additional aid, emphasize that you do care. You care enough to help the person find the best possible support for them.

Here are more specific examples of when to refer:

- You feel in over your head.

- You feel persistently uncomfortable.

- You believe that improvement is "impossible" or the situation is "hopeless."

- The person you visit with says, "Nothing is helping," or what you provide the person isn't helping.

- There is an obvious change in speech and/or appearance.

- The person continues to be so emotional he or she can't communicate.

- There is ongoing deterioration of life (social and physical).

- The person discusses only physical complaints.

- There is a sudden onset of memory confusion.

- You see signs/know of substance abuse.

- The person has hallucinations, delusions or severe pathology.

- The person displays aggression and abuse (verbal and physical).[20]

- The situation seems horrible or unbearable.

- You observe threats of self-harm or harm to others (duty to warn).

In general, if you're unsure, then refer.

How to refer. There may be times when your role as a spiritual care provider is not enough and a referral is needed to help the survivor get further help and more specific assistance from another agency, organization or professional. Do not hesitate to admit that you don't know how to solve a problem. Following are steps you should consider when referring disaster survivors

for additional mental health care.

Before you approach the survivor you wish to refer, understand possible barriers that may be keeping him or her from seeking professional help so that you can offer suggestions for overcoming these barriers.

You should also locate available community resources before talking with disaster survivors. It can be helpful to provide a list of resources and licensed mental health professionals. Making the first contact often is the most difficult part of getting help.

When coming to speak to survivors, ensure privacy by finding a suitable place and do your best to avoid interruptions while you are meeting. This sensitivity to privacy expresses trust, respect and sincerity. Before suggesting a referral, talk about particular behaviors; list the ones you've seen that have concerned you (for example, withdrawal, anger, self-destructive action, lack of sleep or loss of appetite). Ask what the disaster survivor thinks and feels, make sure the person understands what you've said and provide encouragement for any effort they make to reply to the concerns you've voiced.

Continue to be supportive. No matter how much you prepare disaster survivors, you still may not be able to convince them to seek professional help. Keep in mind that there might also be times when you need to make independent referrals, such as when a person or family is unwilling to make the contact or if there is some danger to self or others if action is not taken. In these situations you should take immediate action. Begin the process for an independent referral and help obtain additional care. Remember, in such situations serious concerns about harm to self or others should not be kept confidential.[21]

Preventing and Addressing Helper Burnout and Secondary Trauma

In this section we discuss how to identify burnout and stress in yourself as well as among others, and provide ways to prevent and manage it. Knowing how to identify burnout can help you and others be more helpful in disaster situations over a longer period of time. Thus, the recommendations we provide represent ways to increase care and support for all people engaged in the demanding work of disaster spiritual and emotional care. When reading this section, consider how it applies to you as well as to other volunteers or close peers you might be working with.

Understanding stress, burnout and secondary trauma. Working in disaster situations will inevitably result in experiencing stress. While it may seem manageable at first, experiencing stress over a long period of time without understanding what is causing it or what can be done to relieve it can result in an individual feeling exhausted and not willing or able to work any longer. *Stress* is a state of activation. Under stress, people are energized, more focused and more motivated in response to some demanding situation. That is how stress helps us to manage an unusual situation, by temporarily increasing our resources for action. *Burnout* is a state of deactivation. When we are burned out we have much less energy, motivation or drive. Rather than helping us to adapt, burnout is a withdrawal from the situation that undermines our ability to adapt and grow. This is the essential difference between stress, which is adaptive, and burnout, which undermines adaptation. People who provide care are also at risk for *secondary trauma*, which occurs when we are exposed to a traumatic event experienced by another person. In some cases, the person who has been traumatized may be close to us, or be someone we have great empathy for, and in one conversation we can begin to evidence signs of trauma ourselves. Secondary trauma could happen after seeing a dead body in a disaster zone. The sight may cause you to feel anxious, and it may seem like every time you close your eyes, you can see the body again. The reaction might not happen immediately after the traumatic incident. Instead, you may find yourself remembering the dead body a few months later and experiencing stress then.[22]

Managing stress, burnout and secondary trauma. Uncontrolled stress can lead to many problems. Mild headaches, tight muscles, problems with sleeping or a bad mood can be preludes to much more severe symptoms. Many healthy ways to manage stress exist, but all of them necessitate change—either altering the situation or altering reactions to the situation. The following are descriptions of resilience, building blocks and strategies that will help individuals prevent and manage stress, burnout and secondary trauma.

Draw upon your faith. In our research we have found that our faith can be a powerful source for fostering resilience in disasters and is associated with better overall physical health and mental health. The following is a list of ways to draw upon your faith after a disaster:

- Let your convictions determine your decisions.
- Write in a journal, focusing on your beliefs and goals.
- Make time to read things that inspire you.
- Pray with a group or by yourself.
- Listen to religious music.
- Meditate, whether in an expressly religious way or not.
- Set out religious symbols in your surroundings.
- Stay engaged with your church leaders.
- Maintain your involvement in church activities.
- Converse about spiritual topics through group study of Scripture or in a prayer circle.
- Go to church services and ceremonies and apply yourself to spiritual disciplines.

Monitor yourself. It is important to have accurate knowledge of yourself and the current stressful situation. Knowing how you respond to difficult situations individually (for example, if you get angry easily while in one, or if you tend to work long hours many days in a row) can make it easier when entering into a new situation. One way of preventing trauma or burnout in the future is to ask yourself or your team the following question on a regular basis: Do you have realistic expectations (clear ideas of how often you will work and what you will accomplish over a set amount of time) of yourself and others? You may

enter into a disaster area and have a desire to do whatever is necessary to help those who were affected, regardless of how it will affect your own life. For many Christian volunteers, there may be the additional pressure of "showing Christlike love" or "pouring out everything" to help those in need. It is important to remember that we have limits, and that even Christ retreated for periods of solitude and rest (e.g., Lk 4:42; 5:16). In order to be an effective volunteer over a long period of time, realistic limits must be set.

Create a concrete plan. Changing one's life to improve health often means a change in lifestyle. Establishing a specific plan for making changes in health habits is essential for success. Choose a single area to concentrate on at one time. In making this choice, think about areas in which you want to improve or are most likely to be successful. Progress in one area can help draw you on to continued development. Set a specific goal and separate this goal into pieces that can each be easily managed. Move slowly, focusing on each piece until your goal is achieved. Inform important people in your life about your goals and seek out their support. When needed, procure guidance and professional support. Once you reach your goal, work to maintain your achieved level over time.

Try to find time for leisure. Leisure implies doing things that you take pleasure in (e.g., spending time with family and friends or engaging in hobbies). You can help manage stress by recognizing when you need to take a break. When people are under too much pressure, it's common for them to stop socializing and doing things they enjoy. Part of being healthy is making time for leisure activities among daily responsibilities. Do not neglect what you have enjoyed doing in the past. Doing can serve to make difficult situations in life easier. Such activities may be particularly necessary following a disaster. Though it may be difficult, and you may even feel guilty, it is important to get away from the disaster-affected area when possible. Perhaps this means just getting away for the weekend. At the same time, we recognize this may be difficult, especially early on. So, consider having family or friends from out of town come and visit to spend time with you and offer encouragement.

Engage in physical activities. Exercise is linked to relaxation and well-being. Those who exercise routinely report greater self-esteem and morale as well as a sense of discipline. Exercise helps one feel better, enhancing psychological well-being and relieving symptoms of distress. Regular exercise can aid in renouncing unhealthy habits that hamper exercise (e.g., smokers may cut back or quit because smoking inhibits aerobic exercise). One easy form of exercise is walking. This type of moderate exercise can significantly help with stress management. If you are aiming for improved physical fitness, one ideal exercise program consists of aerobic exercise three to four times per week for twenty to thirty minutes. Spend five to ten minutes warming up beforehand and then cooling down afterward. It's always good to speak with your doctor before starting a new exercise program. For those whose goal includes improved physical fitness, an ideal

exercise program involves aerobic exercise three to four times a week for twenty to thirty minutes, preceded and followed by a five- to ten-minute warm-up and cool-down period, respectively. Consider consulting with your primary care provider before beginning a new exercise program.

Get rest. Different people need different amounts of sleep. If you don't feel rested when you wake up, and you feel sleepy during the day or when you're driving, you may not be getting enough sleep for your body. Other signs include sleeping long past your normal wakeup time when you do not set an alarm. While most people are able to function relatively well when getting less sleep than they need, inadequate sleep can prevent optimal performance and create safety concerns. Common signs of inadequate sleep are irritability, poor concentration and fatigue. Not getting enough sleep can make dealing with stress more challenging, and life stressors can in turn disrupt sleep.

Try to eat healthy. It can be easy to let proper nutrition slide when we are under pressure, but we require the same amount of essential nutrients when under stress. If you are under mental or emotional stress, keep in mind these tips.

- Do not binge or eat only "convenience foods"—take time for eating well.

- Eat a healthy breakfast to help yourself get going before starting your day.

- Many people want comfort foods when they feel stressed. If you feel this craving, look for low-fat or low-calorie versions of these items, and remember to check serving sizes.

- Try to eat only one serving of a given food and eat smaller, more frequent meals.
- Relish your food by sitting down and eating deliberately, concentrating on what you are eating and not another activity.[23]

Conclusion

There is no ministry that does not connect people in some way, and learning the basics of disaster spiritual and emotional care provides skills that can be used by everyone and cuts across programs. Overall, emotional and spiritual care is one of the most prevalent and complicated of needs that disaster survivors have. Yet these needs are often overshadowed by the overwhelming physical damage caused by disasters. With that in mind, what can your church do to help remove the "rubble" from the hearts of those that your disaster ministry is helping? Consider this a part of equipping your efforts even if it is not the focus of the ministry.

Discussion Questions

1. How might your current ministries be adapted in the event of a disaster to address spiritual and emotional needs?

2. Is there a current disaster chaplain network that leaders from your church might connect to in order to receive specialized training and be ready for deployment? If not, could this potentially be a role for your church to take the lead in your community?

3. Are there community approaches to helping, like the example of starting a food court in Japan, that your church might facilitate?

4. What steps will your disaster ministry take to help prevent burnout and secondary trauma among staff and volunteers?

Part Three

Case Studies and Concluding Thoughts

chapter nine

Case Studies in Disaster Ministry

A book of this scope cannot possibly address every approach to ministry, every resource for preparedness or every form of risk. Therefore, stories can help provide additional examples and bring to life the ideas introduced in the preceding chapters. In this chapter we highlight three in-depth cases that delve into how churches and church leaders from around the globe have engaged in disaster ministry. Specifically, we highlight cases from the Philippines, Japan and the United States.

Case 1: Pastoral and Congregational Needs in the Philippines

In September 2013 HDI joined with the Philippine Council of Evangelical Churches and Micah Network to host a gathering of pastors in Manila to discuss disaster ministry.[1] Thanks to support from two US foundations, we were able to allow pastors from very poor and rural communities to join with us. Many of the pastors had never met with their fellow pastors or the agencies that come to the country in response to a disaster. One agency leader remarked that he was used to seeing the same faces over and over at these gatherings, but this was truly unique. As a result of spending a week together, relationships and networks were started that helped these pastors be better prepared for the disaster that struck that November as Typhoon Yolanda.

Two months after the gathering, on November 2, 2013, the Philippines was struck by Typhoon Haiyan (known locally as Typhoon Yolanda), the strongest typhoon to ever strike land, and one of the strongest cyclones ever recorded before it struck land.[2] More than five thousand died and millions were homeless. Nine months later, while providing training for relief workers and pastors in the Philippines, we saw that many people in rural areas had still not been reached by relief efforts. Full recovery was, by some estimates, going to take ten years. However, starting relationships two months earlier, knowing how to contact people and understanding what others were doing made a clear difference in the response to the typhoon. Bishop Efraim

Tendero of PCEC later remarked that those pastors who attended the gathering experienced less conflict during the disaster relief effort and served the communities more efficiently. It was a dramatic example of how preparedness is also about community relationships that are developed well in advance.

During the September gathering we invited thirteen pastors to meet with us individually for an in-depth conversation about their disaster ministry work, what they were learning and the challenges they were facing. Their responses provide insights to the challenges churches face in disaster ministry and how they made, and continue to make, a difference in responding to Typhoon Yolanda.

Pastoral insights. The most frequent and basic challenge faced by the pastors we spoke with was in the theology of church mission. (This may have been primed by our conference, which focused on this issue.) Pastors were very aware of a gap between a traditional view of mission (focusing on conversion) and engaging in disaster ministry (focusing on vulnerability and community). The sense of the people we spoke with was that this was an artificial distinction, but one that was entrenched and challenging to change. Addressing this challenge required helping the church to rethink both missions and disasters.

Disasters are a driving force for collaboration. While some churches may prefer to keep their work within their own congregation, most report finding the needs so huge and overwhelming that in order to accomplish anything they must work with others. However, in order to work with others relationships and communications need to be in place in advance. During disasters, under the stress of trying to respond in a timely way to overwhelming needs, when churches may operate independently of one another, there can be competition between churches (this happens in the United States as well as other places) and an unfortunate waste of time and resources. Knowing your fellow pastors and churches not only makes you better informed, but also makes it more likely that you will cooperate and collaborate.

Pastors described how their experience with disasters was changing the mission of their churches. As people saw the human needs and suffering and began to respond, it was changing them and their church. They told us,

> We reach out to the street families, to the street children, and to those who are basically rejected by the society and basically even some churches [don't] want them to be in the church. That's why this church, my church, was born. Because when I started doing the outreach with the street children, no church wanted to do that.
>
> The outreach in its mission to equip the church for responsive and effective service to the community, connects with the community to keep the spirit of unity and harmony among local churches and with wider church bodies—to serve together in solidarity.
>
> So when it comes to disaster things and all, there is that great need for us to be more inclusive rather than exclusive in the way that we think. We tend to think more about our own issues, about our own issues with the church, the

needs of the church and its members, but forget that in a sense God placed the church in this position with a lot of resources to be able to be a channel of blessing to the others. I'm not saying we are not generous in doing that. In fact our church is very generous in terms of supporting many others, but it's more the change of mindset. To be more proactive and intentional in how we reach out to others. And not just wait for requests and all that.

Our church is trying our best to collaborate with other churches and our mission is to be a catalyst of transformation in the community.

We then explored what pastors say they need for the church to fulfill its mission. Needs varied widely, from material and financial to personnel, training and spiritual needs.

Well, at least, it's very important to have funds and people. We need expertise trainings, more trainings, working on this, understanding the law.

Personally, I need to learn how to network more, but it comes naturally as you learn how to communicate with others and then, you know, how to tap resources we can't see. I know the resources are out there, but how do I tap that? How do I get access? So, I'm not familiar with that.

I think we need to be, other than financial support, other than that, we need to be uplifted, upgraded in our trainings. We need to be more equipped as far as materials is concerned because we don't have materials down there. It's so expensive.

The help we need from the international partners is the rehabilitation and

the, what you call that, to help the people after the disaster. Long-term, long-term help. Especially in that place I told you a while ago in the small community. People there live only in makeshift houses. Every time the flood comes it'll be submerged in the water and you cannot see it anymore. So after three months they'll be back there. So what will happen to the stick, to the sap, and plastic that covers the homes. That is nothing. They will start again.

The discussion of the services provided by churches reveals a diverse mix of relief and development, with an emphasis on getting people out of the very vulnerable situations they are in, and in helping the most vulnerable, which usually means children. There is a recognition that disaster impacts are a cycle of destruction to the most vulnerable, and unless that vulnerability is reduced the cycle will just keep repeating.

Every time there is a calamity like typhoon, floodings, and a lot of people that live along the Manila Bay shoreline, a lot of them get their houses destroyed by the waves and by the strong winds, and every time that there is a calamity like that I'm always there and we're responding even though we're small, through different ways of networking—calling friends, doctors, business people and asking them, "Hey, do you have rice, give something, do you have some construction materials that we could help these families?" and then coordinating with the government, with the social welfare, and some doctors and hospitals and teachers and schools.

We are involved in, during the war in

1990, there was a war in Mindanao in 1990, we responded just after the war and helped the people, specifically the Muslims whose houses were burned during the war, we reconstructed the houses. And, in fact, the group was, the group what that was created, the acronym is ISLAM, Project ISLAM. It stands for: "I Sincerely Love All Muslims." It was so celebrated that it was featured in almost all TV stations in the country, yeah the Project ISLAM. Because we were then building not just the houses of the Muslims that were burned, but we also rebuilt the mosque. Pastors were building the mosque.

We've been counseling them [orphaned children], but I think the problem is so deep that we cannot just push them out or physically take them out from that kind of feeling. Instead, we need to be with them. That's really painful. That is why we have young people ministry there in the rehabilitation center. We are trying to guide them back to the life ministry, but I think the problem is so deep that until this time they are not yet healed.

We also wanted to know if churches target certain groups of people for outreach. Some pastors focus on supporting their staff:

I'm supposed to pastor, shepherd all the pastoral team and ministry heads, plus their individual, they have each an individual ministry team. That's my immediate congregation, if that's what you call it. At the same time, I am also tasked to look after the concerns and the welfare of the individual satellite pastors. There are about twelve now, from twenty and now

it's just about twelve, so that's good news. (laughs) But under the main, we call "core staff," which is the full-time church workers, about forty, aside from the three ministries I mentioned earlier, there are also support ministries.

The more frequent response was to focus on families and children. For example,

It's in Tondo where it's the biggest squatters families—biggest squatters—it's called Baseco area and Parola and Islang Puting Buto. Basically, a lot of number of the street children of Metro Manila are coming from the Tondo area. So, more or less there are about 75,000 street children in Metro Manila, but almost 40 percent of that are from Manila. In Manila, there at least 33,000 homeless families. And so, my church, our church, works there. We reach out to the street families, to the street children, and to those who are basically rejected by the society. There are even some churches that don't want these people around.

What we can learn. Across all of these conversations with Philippine pastors, an important feature stands out that has implications for us all. These pastors were not describing relief work in the usual sense. None of the conversations were about short-term cleanup, though they were doing that. They did not talk about disasters as an unusual event that may not happen again. The underlying theme was about living with disasters. It was about the church needing to help their communities on an ongoing basis. These pastors were discussing examining theology and shifting the understanding of the church because they saw disasters as an ongoing and enduring issue in life, not as an exception to the rule. Put another way, these pastors were recognizing that while Typhoon Yolanda was an extreme example, disasters are part of life in the Philippines, and in order to minister to the community, the church needs to understand how disasters impact life every day. The churches in the Philippines know that Yolanda was the most extreme example yet, but in a country with an average of twenty-six typhoons a year, serving means recognizing that the typhoons are getting more severe, and they are the rule, not the exception. Thus, churches are often confronted with the way the most vulnerable suffer and the need for churches to help their congregations grow so they can serve those who suffer most.

Case 2: Pastors' Views on Church and Community in Post-Disaster Japan

This case study looks at how pastors' views on church and community changed following the 2011 earthquake, tsunami and nuclear meltdown.[3] This case is based on interviews conducted with ten clergy in Japan approximately a year after the disaster. Pastors' responses highlighted a significant shift in the culture of Japanese churches toward collaboration with other congregations and organizations. After introducing the historical and cultural context, which frames the interactions among Japanese churches and their communities, this case study will discuss three main themes that emerged from the pastoral interviews.

Brief description of historical and cul-

tural context. Though some scholars suggest Nestorian Christianity may have entered Japan sometime between the sixth and thirteenth centuries, Christianity's first verifiable appearance in Japan occurred in 1549 with the arrival of Portuguese Jesuits, most notably Francis Xavier. After a brief period of official tolerance, the faith was severely repressed from the end of the sixteenth century through the seventeenth and eighteenth centuries. When Japan was forcibly "opened" for trade in the mid-nineteenth century, Christian missionaries sought to resume the evangelization efforts that had abruptly ceased centuries earlier. Despite initial success and optimism that Japan soon would become a "Christian nation," Christianity failed to spread rapidly in Japan, and today only about 1 percent of Japan's population identifies itself as Christian.

Increased interest in collaborating with other churches and community groups. In contrast to the tendency toward isolation among churches in Japan, a significant development in interchurch and church-community relations can be seen in the recognition by church leaders that relationships with other churches and the local community have value and should be pursued—at least for the purposes of disaster preparation and response. This change can be seen from the fact that, in response to the question, "What do you think you should do as a church about the next earthquake?," 90 percent of the pastors interviewed mentioned strengthening their relationship with the local community, and 70 percent indicated a desire for deeper cooperation among churches.

Such a positive response contrasts historic separation among church groups and suggests that collaboration among churches and their communities is currently viewed more favorably by pastors than traditionally has been the case. Pastors not only regard such partnerships positively but even have taken concrete steps to build relationships with other church and community groups. Two pastors described their participation in networks of church leaders from various denominations. These networks originally were created to strengthen fellowship and advance evangelism, but their members are now considering ways they might adapt these networks to facilitate collaborative disaster relief among churches. Other church leaders described relationships with other congregations from the same denomination.

In times of disaster, denominational leaders utilize these relationships to organize relief efforts to aid congregations in need. Pastors also reported relationships between their congregations and secular groups, although these partnerships generally existed with governmental (as opposed to community) organizations. In many cases, this cooperation is mandated by law, as organizations (including churches) with more than fifty members are required to partner with the government in preparing for disasters by participating in safety training at local fire stations. Besides this mandatory participation, one pastor reported sharing information with his local ward office about the church's disaster resources through a friend who works at that office.

Historical and cultural barriers and challenges to collaboration. Despite this general interest in partnering with other groups, church leaders highlighted a number of barriers to collaboration. A commonly mentioned problem for church-community partnership was that most church members (and sometimes even the pastor himself) do not live in the church's neighborhood but must commute, sometimes from significant distances, to reach the church. Living outside of the community, these church members are unable to participate in activities with church neighbors and so no relationship is developed. In addition, multiple pastors expressed an inability to join their local neighborhood association because of the association's relationship with the local shrine. Dues required of association members support shrine activities, and so church leaders feel caught in a problem with no viable solution: either they join the neighborhood association and give church offerings to the Shinto shrine, or they refuse to compromise their principles and are forced to remain outside of the association.

Additionally, multiple pastors indicated a willingness to cooperate with government-led disaster preparation initiatives but had little to no contact with local community organizations. One pastor said directly that he will follow whatever disaster preparations his local government instructs him to take but will not collaborate with others for any additional disaster relief efforts. He does not see his role as initiating anything outside of what the government is doing. This perspective highlights an interesting view of the church's role in society: the church as subject to the government (at least in matters overseen by the government), obediently fulfilling its role as prescribed by those in power—contrasting the view, for example, of the church working alongside the government as an equal or greater partner.

The interviews thus suggested that church leaders felt comfortable working under the government, with whom there was a clear, hierarchical relationship that would not need to be carefully maintained after the period of disaster training finished. By contrast, pastors were reluctant to attempt building relationships with local community groups and organizations with whom no clearly organized relationship existed and with whom such a relationship would require a regular investment of time and energy. They argued that such horizontal relationships are foreign to Japanese society, in which rigidly hierarchical, vertical relationships are the norm.

Besides these barriers to partnership with the local community, pastors also highlighted a number of challenges to church-church collaboration. One pastor stated that such relationships are complicated by differences in church denomination, size, ethnicity and other related factors. Other church leaders, particularly young pastors, described an inability for churches to pursue partnerships because of social rules that limit the influence of young, visionary leaders. Among Japanese churches, leaders with a vision to advance collaboration among congregations are usually members of the young generation

of pastors. These young leaders must defer, however, to the authority of older pastors, most of whom lack the vision, initiative and energy to pursue such goals. This age-related difference highlighted age as the variable that created the greatest divergence among responses. Differences in location, denomination and church size did not consistently show the same effect as age, which separated pastors into two distinct camps: the elderly pastors who boldly promoted their respective congregations' independent disaster relief efforts, and the younger church leaders who regularly highlighted the need for greater collaboration among churches and with community groups in disaster preparations.

Recommendations for overcoming barriers. In order to overcome these barriers to partnership, the pastors suggested various methods of collaboration that would address the unique cultural challenges they face. In regard to interchurch partnership, a common suggestion was to have a third-party organization (e.g., the Japan Evangelical Association) organize a church network. Such an arrangement would address the impasse between younger pastors with vision but lacking authority and older pastors with authority but a lack of initiative for church cooperation. In addition, by having a third-party organization take the lead in creating such a network, the problems created by needing to establish a hierarchy would be mitigated. The risk of power struggles would be reduced if network leadership came from outside the denominations of churches and was clearly established from the beginning.

As a concrete illustration, shortly after completing these interviews, HDI, working closely with the JEA and DRC Net (Disaster Relief Christian Network, an association of Japanese Christian leaders working together to advance disaster relief work), created a disaster-focused social networking website for church and organization leaders involved in disaster preparation and response. This online network offers a platform for church-church and church-organization collaboration in a way that reduces cultural barriers to partnership by enabling leaders to interact through the comfortable distance of the Internet, limiting the burden of relational responsibilities, and having the JEA and DRC Net (with support from HDI) facilitate interaction as a third party.

In addition, in order to encourage church-community collaboration, one pastor offered his own church as an example of how to cooperate with municipal organizations effectively. This church is an example of a group cooperating with the local government by attending the mandatory safety training and is an interesting example of cooperating "appropriately," culturally speaking: cooperating with other organizations with whom the relational hierarchy is clear and well-established, but not initiating cooperation with churches from other denominations, secular community groups or other groups with which there is not already an established relationship. Attempting to begin relationships with these groups likely feels too inappropriate, tiresome and uncomfortable, since there is no clear protocol for how to relate. Therefore, this church serves as an example of the importance of having well-established ties and a clear hierarchical structure before attempting collaboration.

Summary. In summary, pastors expressed interest in partnering with others for disaster preparation and relief to an extent that contrasts prior isolation among Japanese churches. This willingness to cooperate represents a major change in the culture of Japanese churches with respect to church and community relationships. However, this vision is promoted primarily by younger church leaders and is not always held by older, more influential pastors. Additionally, several other barriers exist to church-community partnerships, including church leaders and members not living in the church neighborhood, an unwillingness to belong to community associations in which dues would be given to the local shrine, and entrenched cultural rules that impede the creation of "horizontal" relationships (i.e., relationships among peer organizations in which there is no clear hierarchy). Collaboration with the government has been somewhat easier than with community groups because of the absence of these barriers. In regard to interchurch partnerships, perceived barriers such as differences in size, ethnic makeup and denomination may be overcome if a third-party organization (particularly one with an equal relationship to all the parties involved) facilitates collaboration through communication tools (e.g., networking websites) and events (e.g., trainings and conferences) that gradually but consistently bring churches together for a common goal.

Case 3: Examination of a Denomination's Response to Hurricane Katrina

This case study examines the denominational response of a major Christian denomination after Hurricane Katrina along the Mississippi Gulf Coast and New Orleans, Louisiana.[4] We conducted in-depth interviews with twenty different clergy significantly affected by Hurricane Katrina. This case study highlights what the clergy viewed as the most helpful aspects of the denomination's response as well as areas perceived to need change or growth. Following these findings, a set of recommendations are provided that integrate suggestions offered in regard to all levels of denominational assistance to individual churches for disaster preparation and recovery.

Most helpful aspects of regional response. Participants described the helpfulness of their regional office's financial assistance. The level of financial support varied from church to church, based on a number of factors, such as level of damage to church, location of church (in highly affected versus less affected areas) and opportunities for social outreach programming. For instance, one clergy member reported, "My congregation received over $172,000 from their regional office." Others reported that their regional leadership provided contributions to their operating budgets and helped make up for deficits in their church budgets. Participants reported how helpful the protected funding of their salary, benefits and pension was to them. These leaders and disaster ministry representatives also said that financial assistance given to hire temporary staff was very useful. A number of these participants

shared that they were grateful for the leniency with discretionary funds that was shown, which reportedly made it easier for them to attend to the needs of their congregation and community more immediately. Similarly, a few participants noted that the regional office's relaxed regulations for purchasing property were useful in the recovery process. However, it should also be noted that a few of the disaster ministry representatives stated that they felt as though some of the regional office's financial assistance was "lopsided. . . . I felt like some of the camps got all this funding and we had to just scrape by with what we could. Most of our budget came from us raising our own money."

Participants positively discussed their regional office's level of support and availability. Frequent stops and visits by their respective regional directors were commonly reported. According to participants, their regional directors and regional office staff showed empathy for disaster reactions and sought to understand and relate to the stresses associated with being clergy members in the aftermath of Hurricane Katrina. Further, participants described the response of their regional leadership as "immediate, concentrated, community focused and socially focused." Overall, participants stated that their regional directors and regional offices helped facilitate a sense of security and safety by tending to the personal needs of clergy.

Although the regional office staff was challenged by their own personal losses, most participants reported that regional officials took care of clergy and tried to make sure adequate recovery time was given.

Participants also expressed that regional officials and staff made their presence and support known by opening lines of communication in a nonhierarchical manner. One participant recalled an experience with his presiding regional director: "He and I cried together in front of the altar at our little church. Just knowing that he was the presiding [regional director], that he was there, that he came to see firsthand what our area was . . . he was present, and cared." Finally, most participants asserted they were encouraged by the support and collaboration shown between and across the various regional offices that were affected by Hurricane Katrina.

Participants also reported that they found their regional office's help in developing partner church relationships very useful to the recovery process. "Partner [churches] all over the United States said 'we will help you, we will pray for you, come see us, we'll give you some money.'" These participants said they and their congregations benefited from the national support network that evolved with the help of their regional offices. Further, publicity efforts of these offices to raise awareness among the partner church programs were thought to have led to additional forms of support (e.g., spiritual, financial and social). Participants also discussed receiving significant help from other churches in their own regions.

Participants noted that they benefited from their regional offices hiring specialized staff to offer support and expertise for responding to Hurricane Katrina. For example, one church leader stated, "Our [regional director] used resources wisely,

such as putting people in place and hiring for new positions—we needed all the help we could get." Examples of helpful hiring and expansion included creation of counseling pastor positions, staff to address mental health issues and new departments to handle future responses. The hiring of counseling pastors resonated highly among participants. "The [regional director] appointed a pastor who has extensive counseling background to work with the clergy and families of [churches] here on the coast—our Canon Minister was fabulous." Placing clergy on the coast to address the mental health issues of affected church leaders was vital, as evidenced by this participant's recollection: "I just think a big thing that was important was [that the regional offices placed clergy] on the coast to sort of address those [psychological] needs."

Participants said their denomination's regional offices led social justice efforts to address inequalities (e.g., racial and social economic status inequalities) made obvious by Hurricane Katrina. For instance, one participant stated, "The [denomination] has become more of an advocate for the poor and disadvantaged since the storm in our community." Another church leader noted, "Even though we were trying to hold our own families together and trying to find places to live . . . we were feeding the hungry, we were clothing the naked, and we were taking care of the people that no one else would take care of." Participants also reported that their regional offices were very helpful in ensuring that their congregants received the specialized care they needed following Hurricane Katrina through services such as case management, which has "morphed itself into [the denomination's community services agency], which was the direct result of beginning to just take care of folks after Hurricane Katrina." Finally, participants' representatives alike discussed how the aforementioned efforts had increased awareness of the denomination in Mississippi and Louisiana.

Regional response considerations for growth. Participants said that they could have benefited from more fundraising assistance from their regional offices following Hurricane Katrina. One participant reported, "We just didn't have the capacity to fundraise with everything that was going on. If there had been a centralized group regionally helping to raise funds, that would have been a game changer for us." Participants also indicated that they felt the regional office response was lacking. "I did not feel like I benefited very much from any of the monetary assistance or personnel that came down that went through our regional offices." Participants reported they experienced competition for regional resources among churches. Participants also stated they thought more could have been done to prepare clergy whose churches did not experience severe damage for volunteer work in their denominational region. One participant expressed that the amount of volunteers was immense. "We were almost overwhelmed by those kind of offers to the point that . . . trying to manage that was difficult." Participants reported that they believed some of the disaster ministries that acted as distribution centers and helped house volunteers could have been more centrally lo-

cated geographically. These participants thought that a few of the sites could have been positioned better to enhance proximity to a wider range of churches. Other notable findings include participants who indicated that they thought the response of the denomination's regional office was centered too much on areas in which the news media focused—"The relief aid and response needs to go beyond just where the television camera is."

Most helpful aspects of the denomination's national response and the denominational relief and development agency's response. Many helpful aspects of the denomination's national response came through the national director's office, the denomination's pension committee and the denomination's relief and development agency. Participants reported they benefited from time away from areas affected by Hurricane Katrina through experiences like postdisaster conferences. One participant said, "The conference was seen as a success. It was helpful for processing, and provided a guiltless environment and detachment from Hurricane Katrina." Participants also stated that having their pension and related benefits covered as extremely helpful. These leaders stated that knowing their pension was being taken care of helped sustain their disaster relief efforts. Support in the form of providing additional staffing and administrative support was also identified by participants as a helpful response. Examples of helpful staff support included the addition of counseling pastors, mental health professionals, church assistants and administrative oversight offered by the denominational relief and development agency. "The new position that the national church created [counseling pastor] was one wonderful piece."

Participants stated encouraging and supporting volunteers was one of the most significant contributions made by the broader national church leadership and the denomination's relief and development agency. One church leader noted, "The number of volunteers who were motivated to come in was just really heartwarming and astounding." Connected to this, participants thought that the development of disaster relief ministries and volunteer camps, for adults as well as youth, were noted as examples of this form of support. Participants thought the national director's office did a positive job helping to raise awareness about Hurricane Katrina–related issues and needs.

Several church leaders noted that such efforts helped to maintain a "national spotlight" on the ongoing recovery efforts through local and national media attention. "The publicity that the national church kept on the situation was very helpful because it kept it in front of people so that when I did go and make pleas for assistance for the church or for the people in the area, it was easy because people were aware of it. . . . I could give them the personal side of things and some of the down-on-the-ground reports." Participants described the denomination's national church office and relief and development arm's fundraising and collection of donations as very helpful. One participant stated that "the money that came in from [the relief and development agency] was very pos-

itive, and it was a huge amount." Participants also brought attention to the national denominational leadership's role in helping support regional offices that were affected by Hurricane Katrina. Finally, participants reported that their churches benefited from funding that was used to help reclaim buildings damaged by Hurricane Katrina. In most cases this came from grants that were issued to help congregations attend to community needs, such as repairing a building that was used as a soup kitchen following the storm.

Considerations for growth in light of responses by the denomination's national office and its relief and development agency. Participants reported there seemed to be some confusion or lack of clarification about how the denomination's relief and development agency would allow funds to be used. For example, some clergy reported that they had heard about people who had given to this agency thinking that their donations would assist with rebuilding churches and buildings. However, these leaders went on to say that they did not think that donations for rebuilding churches were in line with the giving policies of the agency. Some of the church leaders perceived the agency as having had accepted designated funds without appropriately disseminating the funds. One clergy member recalled one such instance: "I talked to people who called and said, 'We sent money to the national church for you.' It never got to us." However, according to representatives from the relief and development agency, donors could specify that their donations be designated for specific uses and even specific churches; the problem appeared to be that some donors did not explicitly designate (or did not know to designate) how their donations were to be allotted, which may have complicated dispersion of funds and perceptions in some instances. This would appear to have significant implications for affecting future giving.

Participants reported that they thought it would have been helpful for the national church leadership to place more emphasis on funding the rebuilding of churches. "A change in the use of funds for [denominational relief and development], where it could help the brick and mortar of churches postdisaster, would have been incredibly helpful to us." Another church leader reflected on the current status of his church: "This is three years after the storm; it still feels like the war zone. . . . If the denomination wants their congregations to survive, they've got to help them open back up." Representatives from the national denominational office and the denomination's relief and development agency reported that there was not enough funding available to support large building projects across all churches affected if the national office was going to be able to sustain a long-term recovery presence.

Thus, the representatives who participated in the study reported that they had sought to find ways to leverage the funding that was raised, and that funding programs was one of the ways thought to be able to make a long-term difference in the lives of those affected by Hurricane Katrina. For example, a plethora of socially focused outreach ministries were developed to bring healing to those affected by the

storm. Working with credit unions in both Mississippi and Louisiana to offer bridge loans (that is, financial assistance to cover the "gap" left between insurance payouts, down payment and actual amount needed to receive a housing loan) to help affected residents get back into affordable housing was a novel approach also highlighted. Those interviewed from the national church office and the denominational relief and development agency reported that they recognized the importance and need for funding to help in rebuilding churches and buildings destroyed. However, they expressed concerns that if buildings had been emphasized over programs, then fewer people would have been helped overall.

Participants in this study frequently talked about how integral volunteers have been and continue to be to the recovery process. For instance, one church leader said, "The church sent volunteers and were here [New Orleans] to help before anyone else, even before the government. And you know what, they are the only ones still around helping." Still, church leaders said that they were overwhelmed by the additional responsibilities of having to oversee volunteers and would have liked to see more support managing the volunteers at the local church level.

Fewer participants reported that they had experienced some political tensions during contacts with others from the broader national-level denominational church. One clergy member gave the example of a verbal disagreement emerging after a visitor noticed his conference banner hanging in the church. He said,

"We should have been coming together, more than ever, not bickering over church politics." Another church leader stated, "I felt like a few of them [church volunteers and leaders] were there because it might help them move through the political ranks of the church faster."

Summary

The following is a series of recommendations that were garnered from participants for strengthening future responses by their denomination, both at a local and national level. Encourage disaster preparedness at all levels of the church nationally (preparedness was stressed not only for churches in regions more at risk for disasters, but for all churches). Continue to be involved in long-term awareness campaigns following disasters. Keep local and national attention on disaster needs and relief efforts. Increase planning and development of protocols for volunteer management during disasters at the local church level. Provide additional resources to help organize rebuilding and stewardship campaigns to raise money for repairing or rebuilding churches affected by disasters.

Conclusion

Though each of these case studies highlights different disasters from different parts of the world, there are several themes that emerge. First, people turn to the church in times of crisis. Even if the participants' churches had not planned on responding to disasters, each were called

upon to help after their respective disasters. Second, disasters create unique opportunities for churches to expand their ministries to help the vulnerable. The disasters all brought the vulnerabilities and injustices that already existed in each of their communities to the forefront. In some cases, if it were not for the local church, these needs might not have been addressed. Third, the need created by these disasters far exceeded the capacity of any one church to address it. This meant that the churches had to learn how to rely upon one another and upon others, such as government agencies and nonprofit organizations. Fourth, doing disaster ministry meant doing more than just disaster relief work. The narrative studies show that effective disaster ministry starts with getting prepared and continues all the way through long-term recovery. They also highlight that churches are often the first to respond and the last still helping with recovery.

Discussion Questions

1. What themes did you notice that cut across each of these cases?

2. Do you notice any cultural differences that may have influenced how these church leaders and congregations carried out their disaster ministry work?

3. What resonated with you most from these cases and why?

4. Were there challenges shared by these church leaders that you had not thought about before? How might you address such issues?

chapter ten

Conclusion

Many churches, like many people, think, "Disasters can never happen to me." After Hurricane Camille, people said the storm was a "once-in-a-lifetime storm." After Hurricane Katrina it was, "This was a once-in-a-hundred-years storm." And after a recent trip to Japan we heard, "This was a once-in-a-thousand-years disaster." No one likes to think that bad things might happen. It is human nature. But this makes us vulnerable. It is not necessary to adopt a mentality of doom or gloom, or repeat the mistakes of fear many churches embraced in preparation for Y2K (otherwise known as the "Millennium bug," where people feared technology would fail, assuming that computers wouldn't be able to distinguish the year 2000 from the year 1900). If your church doesn't already have a ministry in place to address catastrophes, crises and emergencies—the time to start is now. Or perhaps you read this book because your community recently recovered from a disaster. As the examples show, "lightning can strike twice." Though we hope with you that the worst has already come, it's time to reflect on the lessons you've learned

and to adapt for possible future disasters.

As highlighted throughout this handbook, the local church plays an important role in helping congregations and communities prepare, respond to and recover from disasters. Even if your church has never thought about its role in a disaster, if an emergency strikes your community, people are going to turn to you for help.[1] Engaging in disaster ministry can lead to new ministry and fellowship opportunities. Accordingly, we have sought to help prepare you with best practices for developing general plans that can be incorporated into other ministries and examples of specialized plans for the disasters you are most likely to face in your area.

We submit that preparing your own congregation is the best place to start even if your aim is to serve your community. By strengthening your ministries in general you are preparing yourself to be in a better position to respond effectively by "pivoting" into disaster mode. This in turn will help your congregation be more resilient in the face of adversity. It will also help you be better positioned for restoring critical ministries and getting your operational infrastructure back up and running. We have seen some churches get so enthusiastic about serving in disasters that they end up forgetting their original mission and purpose. This makes every part of the disaster ministry process more difficult. Decisions become more difficult, and the focus of efforts becomes skewed because they lack an anchor. Do not abandon your congregation's calling. Rather, we would argue a more effective way to respond is to build upon your mission and purpose. Start with strengthening your congregation's regular ministries and then add specialized ministries as you are able.

As you move to implement the lessons you've learned, remember to avoid the temptation to develop a "cookbook" approach to creating your disaster ministry. Each congregation has its own history, culture and approach to ministry. Risks also vary from region to region, and congregation to congregation. Therefore, congregational emergency plans need to meet the unique needs of local congregations and communities. Disaster ministry plans also need to address state and local safety laws. Other plans can serve as useful models, but what is effective for a large inner-city congregation where the population is concentrated may be ineffective for a rural church where congregations and first responders are far apart.

Further, your disaster ministry needs to take into account and leverage your congregation's unique talents, calling and gifting. The churches we have seen who have developed the most effective disaster ministries were the ones that started small and built on their strengths. This allowed

them to take a developmental approach, grow in their vision, add appropriate resources and sustain their work. Thus, it is important to begin by matching your congregation resources with specific goals. Then identify gaps in resources (goals without a matching resource), and take steps to address each gap. This should also take into account current congregation and community resources needed.

As you can see throughout the handbook, the ways people and their congregations help in disasters are more varied than the disasters themselves—the possibilities are endless. However, before you start, it is important that you are prepared to maintain your ministry once you launch it. All ministries face the question of how to sustain over time. This is especially true when a disaster ministry is created in reaction to a rare or extreme current event that has gotten a lot of attention. In general, a disaster ministry is more difficult to sustain over time when:

- It is developed in isolation from the other programs or ministries of the congregation.

- It depends on the energy of one or a few people.

- It is not clearly aligned with the mission of the congregation.

- It requires resources (e.g., money) that may not be available in the future.

- It is competing with other programs in your congregation for volunteer time and resources.

- The benefits of the program take a long time to appear, or never appear.

The time to think about how your program will last is when you are just starting. It is more likely to succeed over time when you think about whether the need for the program is a reaction to a crisis. What will happen when the crisis is past? Consider this before you start. There are other things to think about at the onset of starting your disaster ministry. In general, your disaster ministry is more likely to last when:

• It has clear, open and continuing support from congregation members.

• It has clear, reasonable expectations for what the project will produce and what people will do.

• The disaster ministry team takes time to do thoughtful planning.

• The disaster ministry team clarifies their assumptions about the need for the program and checks to see if they are true.

• Growth is managed so it does not grow out of control as people react to a crisis.

• There is a plan for regular communication with the congregation.

• If resources are needed, there is a plan for where they will come from after the crisis is over.

• It clearly supports and enhances the overall mission of the congregation.

• It is combined with existing congregational organizational systems and structures, including leadership structure, training structures and support systems (financial management, recruitment, committees, programs, etc.).

• It can become part of or support existing ministries.

• It provides a way for people to see that their work has benefits (visible and timely benefit from their efforts).

The "pot of gold" or the ultimate achievement in disaster ministry is when it becomes part of the culture of the church, part of what your members say, "This is what we are about. We do this because of who we are." Creating this level of commitment requires two basic things. First, the ministry must express the basic faith values of the members. Cleaning up after a disaster is a very good thing to do, but cleaning up is more than being a good neighbor when it is a part of a ministry that seeks out those who have been overlooked, disadvantaged or who bear an excess burden. Then it is also a ministry of justice and expresses a core faith value of the church. And not just that, but there are other core faith values, including mercy, sacrifice and more. People want to put their faith values into action, and any ministry that clearly expresses that opportunity will connect with people in a basic way. This leads to the second basic requirement, making the link between the ministry and faith.

When people get up in front of the congregation on a Sunday morning and describe a ministry and how that ministry is an expression of what the church believes, their testimony makes the connection for people between faith and action. As people listen, at some level they think, *That is who we are* and *That is what I believe and stand for.* When you make your disaster ministry known to others, it is essential to link it to what the church believes and how it is putting those beliefs into action. When that connection is made for people, when they see the ministry as putting the best of who they are into action, they will become engaged. As the number of people who make that connection grows, you will become the church that does disaster ministry, the church that is prepared, the church that seeks out and serves the most vulnerable, because that is who you are. At that point, the ministry becomes self-sustaining.

Our hope for this handbook is that you will be able to take the lessons you've learned throughout to help you get started in developing, sustaining and growing your disaster ministry. We believe part of the calling for the local church described throughout the Scriptures is to minister to the vulnerable and to care for those in need.[2] As a result, we believe that disaster ministries should focus on people—the congregants and community members—with an emphasis on serving those with the greatest need. People who have fewer resources, fewer connections with other people or a history of struggling with life's problems are likely less resilient (or more vulnerable). They may also require additional assistance through coaching, social support or guidance with planning and decision making.

In summary, disasters represent an opportunity for the church to, in a very real and tangible way, serve as the hands and feet of Christ.[3] *Though disasters reveal injustices, disaster ministries reveal God's love, mercies and grace.*

Discussion Questions

1. What was the biggest takeaway you had from reading this book?

2. What is one small step you can take toward starting a disaster ministry?

3. How might you plan to sustain your disaster ministry after it has launched?

4. If your disaster ministry were successful, what would that look like?

5. What is the long-term vision for your disaster ministry?

Part Four

Tools for Planning and Implementation

Introduction

The following tools provide step-by-step directions, resources and exercises for making your congregation safer and better prepared for a disaster. Disaster planning, training and manuals can easily become ends in themselves unless they are linked to key aims and activities, so we start with helping your congregation set goals and vision. We recognize that not every congregation will need or be able to complete each section. We would encourage your congregation to consider taking a developmental approach to completing the following steps. Start small and with the sections that seem to most naturally fit your congregation's needs, size, mission and vision. After you successfully complete a section, then move on to the next most obtainable goal, and so on.

Congregation Preparedness Plan

Church Information and Approval Page

_____

Church Name

_____

Address

_____

City   State   Zip

_____

Telephone Number

_____

Email Address

Date plan was created: _____

Plan approved by: _____

Plan Review:

Date: _____   Approved by: _____

         _____   _____

         _____   _____

Congregation Disaster Mission

INSTRUCTIONS: Define the purpose of this plan and your congregation's role in the event of an emergency. Examples include:

To ensure the continuation or quick resumption of worship services.

To provide care and support to disaster victims (congregants and community members).

To provide services/resources to help in the community's recovery from emergency (consider what services/resources you plan to provide).

Purpose of Church Plan

_____

_____

_____

_____

_____

_____

_____

_____

_____

_____

Congregational Goals

INSTRUCTIONS: In this section, identify, as a congregation, what you want to accomplish after a disaster, in support of your congregation's disaster mission. This is a definition of what you will strive to accomplish after a disaster; the specific steps to accomplish these goals will be defined later in the plan. Examples of goals may include:

Ensure the safety of older and disabled members of the congregation.

Provide an effective relief ministry to the local community after a disaster.

Reestablish Sunday services as soon as possible postdisaster.

List of Congregational Goals

1)

2)

3)

4)

5)

Building Description

Facility Features

Occupancy type (church, office building, school, etc.)
Total square footage
Year built/date of most recent renovation
Number of stories (Is there a basement?)
Type of construction
Insurance company
Describe any unique features (inside or outside)

NOTE: Attach any floor plans of the facility at the end of the document.

Building Supplies and Safety

Emergency Supplies and Equipment Locations

1. Portable radios and extra batteries:

2. Emergency first-aid supplies:

3. Flashlights and extra batteries:

4. Stored drinking water:

5. Emergency (3-day) food supply:

6. Basic tool kit:

7. Fire alarm system:

   Location of fire alarm:

   Location of fire extinguishers:

   If system monitored by outside agency, name and phone:

   Sprinkler system (water flow valves and standpipes, including tamper alarms):

8. Exits: Information on fire escapes (type and location):

   Information on fire doors (if applicable):

Utility Shutoffs and Tools

1. Main gas valve:

2. Crescent wrench or gas shutoff tools:

3. Main water valve:

4. Electrical fuse box/circuit breaker:

5. Emergency or portable generator (if applicable):

Inventory of Neighborhood Resources

1. Where can you rent or borrow a generator?

2. Where is the nearest medical treatment facility? (Attach driving and walking directions.)

3. Where is the nearest fire station?

4. Where is the nearest police station?

5. Where can you go for additional water?

6. Where can you go for additional food supplies?

7. Where can you go for additional medical supplies, medicines and special equipment?

Disaster Ministry Coordinator (DMC)

Disaster Ministry Coordinator (DMC) and Backup DMC Contact Information

The DMC for our congregation in an emergency is:

_____

Name

_____

Telephone number   Alternate number

_____

Work email address   Home email address

In the absence of the DMC, the first alternate DMC is:

_____

Name

_____

Telephone number   Alternate number

_____

Work email address   Home email address

In the absence of the first alternate DMC, the second alternate DMC is:

_____

Name

_____

Telephone number   Alternate number

_____

Work email address   Home email address

The authorized church emergency spokesperson (if different from DMC) is:

_____

Name

_____

Telephone number   *Alternate number*

_____

Work email address   *Home email address*

Disaster Ministry Team

Team Member Contact and Skill Information

_____

Name

_____

Position

_____

Key responsibilities

_____

Home address   *State*   *Zip*

_____

Home phone

_____

Cell phone

_____

Social networking information

_____

Work email address

_____

Home email address

_____

Emergency contact/Relationship

_____

Emergency contact phone number   *Alternate number*

Do you and your family have an emergency preparedness plan?   ☐ Yes   ☐ No

Do you and your family have an emergency preparedness kit?   ☐ Yes   ☐ No

In an emergency situation would you continue to work assigned duties?   ☐ Yes   ☐ No

In an emergency situation would you be willing to work additional days or hours?   ☐ Yes   ☐ No

In an emergency situation would you be able to work from your home?   ☐ Yes   ☐ No

With personal protective equipment (PPE), would you be willing to work with individuals who have a communicable disease?   ☐ Yes   ☐ No

Certifications: ☐ LPN/RN   ☐ CPR   ☐ First Aid
                       ☐ Emergency Medical Technician   ☐ Other

Church Staff and Leadership

Church Staff Contact and Skill Information

Name

Position

Key responsibilities

Home address   *State*   *Zip*

Home phone

Cell phone

Work email address

Home email address

Emergency contact/Relationship

Emergency contact phone number   *Alternate number*

Do you and your family have an emergency preparedness plan?   ☐ Yes   ☐ No

Do you and your family have an emergency preparedness kit?   ☐ Yes   ☐ No

In an emergency situation would you continue to work assigned duties?   ☐ Yes   ☐ No

In an emergency situation would you be willing to work additional days or hours?   ☐ Yes   ☐ No

In an emergency situation would you be able to work from your home?   ☐ Yes   ☐ No

With personal protective equipment (PPE), would you be willing to work with individuals who have a communicable disease?   ☐ Yes   ☐ No

Certifications: ☐ LPN/RN   ☐ CPR   ☐ First Aid
                     ☐ Emergency Medical Technician   ☐ Other

Taken with permission from Bloomington Public Health. L. Brodsky, M. Drews, K. Henslee, N. Kafumbe and M. Schweizer, "Ready, Set, Go! Faith Community Emergency Preparedness Toolkit." Non-exclusive permission to photocopy for congregational disaster preparedness use is granted by Bloomingdale Public Health, 1800 West Old Shakopee Road, Bloomington, MN 55431, www.bloomingtonmn.gov. Permission is limited to non-commercial print use in English language. All rights reserved. See permissions page for full terms.

Volunteers

Volunteer Contact and Skill Information

_____

Name

_____

Position

_____

Key responsibilities

_____

Home address   State   Zip

_____

Home phone

_____

Cell phone

_____

Work email address

_____

Home email address

_____

Emergency contact/Relationship

_____

Emergency contact phone number   Alternate number

Do you and your family have an emergency preparedness plan?   ☐ Yes   ☐ No

Do you and your family have an emergency preparedness kit?   ☐ Yes   ☐ No

In an emergency situation would you continue to work assigned duties?   ☐ Yes   ☐ No

In an emergency situation would you be willing to work additional days or hours?   ☐ Yes   ☐ No

In an emergency situation would you be able to work from your home?   ☐ Yes   ☐ No

With personal protective equipment (PPE), would you be willing to work with individuals who have a communicable disease?   ☐ Yes   ☐ No

Certifications: ☐ LPN/RN   ☐ CPR   ☐ First Aid
                     ☐ Emergency Medical Technician   ☐ Other

Risk Assessment

INSTRUCTIONS: Evaluate the potential for each event and its potential severity among the following possible emergency events using the scale below. Assume each event occurs at the worst possible time (i.e., during peak gathering times).

Evaluate Risk Factors

PROBABILITY	HUMAN IMPACT	PROPERTY IMPACT	WORKFLOW IMPACT
Likelihood this event will occur	Possibility of death or injury to your staff or your members	Physical losses and damages to your facility and/or vehicles	Interruption of services

Rank the following events accordingly for each category and then add them together to determine your risk for each specific event: High=3, Moderate=2, Low=1, None=0.

Possible Emergency Events	PROBABILITY	HUMAN IMPACT	PROPERTY IMPACT	WORKFLOW IMPACT	Total Risk
Extreme temps—cold					
Extreme temps—heat					
Thunderstorm					
Tornado/ Straight line winds					
Severe winter storm					
Flood—internal					
Flood—external					
Fire—internal					
Fire—external					

Possible Emergency Events	PROBABILITY	HUMAN IMPACT	PROPERTY IMPACT	WORKFLOW IMPACT	Total Risk
Medical— Infectious disease (e.g., Pandemic Influenza)					
Mass casualty— trauma					
Electrical failure/ Power outage					
Criminal disorder					
Civil disorder					
Bomb threat					
Labor action/ strike					
Supply shortage (e.g., food, water)					
HAZMAT (chemical spill)—internal					
HAZMAT (chemical spill)—external					
Radiological— internal					
Radiological— external					
Terrorism— biological					

Possible Emergency Events	PROBABILITY	HUMAN IMPACT	PROPERTY IMPACT	WORKFLOW IMPACT	Total Risk
Terrorism—chemical					
Terrorism—nuclear					
Terrorism—radiological					
Water contamination or shortage					
Transportation problems					
Motor vehicle accident					
Train derailment					
Other:					
Other:					

Score Ranges:

High Risk=9-12, Moderate Risk=5-8, Low Risk=1-4, No Risk=0

Based on this assessment, the following events are most likely to be of concern in our organization:

Communication Plan

INSTRUCTIONS: Fill in each of the boxes below to help develop procedures that will assist your congregation in responding promptly, accurately and confidently during an emergency in the hours and days that follow. Be sure to tailor your procedures to the many different groups in your congregation that must be reached with information specific to their interests and needs.

Risk Communication Strategies

What should you communicate?	To whom are you communicating? (e.g., congregation, staff, local government)	Who should communicate the message? (e.g., Disaster Ministry Coordinator, pastor)	How should it be communicated? (e.g., electronically, phone call/tree, mail)	Preparatory actions (e.g., talking points, key messages, training)
Organizational status				
Damage assessment				
Services offered or service changes				
Funds or supplies needed				
Volunteers needed				
Others needed				
Other:				
Other:				

Directions for remote voicemail:

_____

_____

_____

_____

Directions for remote email:

_____

_____

_____

_____

If phones are not working, our backup communication plan is as follows (include provisions for land line and cellular phones):

_____

_____

_____

_____

Designate one remote phone number where an emergency message can be recorded, and be sure that all congregation members know that number and understand its use.

Number:

Responsible party:

Alternate responsible party:

Additional communication directions:

_____

_____

_____

_____

_____

_____

_____

Sample Calling Tree

(Note: Some churches may have a prayer chain that can be adapted for this purpose.)

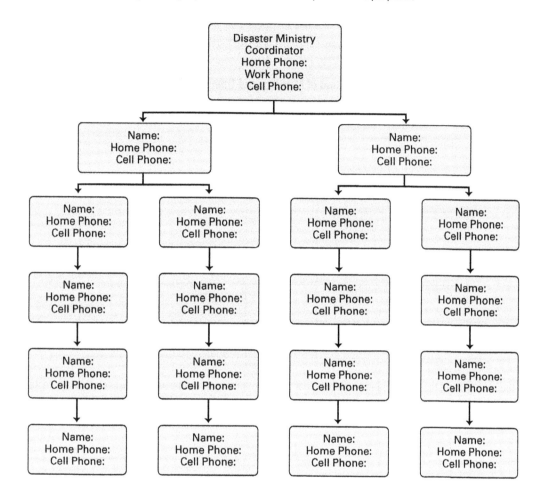

Continuity of Ministries and Services

Evaluation of Ministry and Operations

Ministry/Service/Program	Suspend (x)	Maintain (x)	Supplies/Resources needed to maintain

List the supplies and resources needed to keep your church operating and alternative ways to obtain those items.

Supply or resource needed   **Alternative source for obtaining resource**

_____

_____

_____

_____

_____

_____

Church plan of succession (List, by position or title, which staff member or volunteer is next in line to assume overall authority following a disaster.)

1. _____

2. _____

3. _____

4. _____

List of signatories on bank accounts (in the event that the primary signatory is unavailable).

1. _____

2. _____

3. _____

4. _____

Specify area for involvement during an emergency.

_____

_____

_____

_____

_____

_____

Offsite Storage of Important Documents and Vital Records

_____
Organization name

_____
Address

_____
City   *State*   *Zip*

_____
Telephone number

Vital Records may include but are not limited to:

□ articles of incorporation   □ financial statements (bank accounts, credit cards)

□ artwork (e.g., stationery, logo)   □ 501(c)(3)

□ blank checks and account information   □ insurance information

□ board minutes and rosters   □ inventory of organization equipment

□ bylaws   □ leases/deeds

□ client records   □ licenses

□ computer passwords   □ mission statement

□ contracts   □ personnel records/payroll information

□ corporate seal   □ photographs of the facility and key equipment

□ diagram of building layout   □ tax exemption status certificate

□ donor records   □ vendor records

□ emergency plan   □ volunteer records

Other documents:

1. _____

2. _____

3. _____

4. _____

Offsite Storage of Vital Electronic Records

How often are electronic records backed up? _____

Backed-up records are kept at:

_____
Name

_____
Address

_____
City   *State*   *Zip*

_____
Telephone number

If accounting and payroll records are destroyed, continuity will be provided by the following:

1. _____

2. _____

3. _____

Backed-up electronic records include the following:

1. _____

2. _____

3. _____

4. _____

5. _____

6. _____

7. _____

Neighboring Congregations or Agencies Providing Additional/Backup Services

(Note: Churches are encouraged to adopt a "sister" church in their community and out of region who agrees to come to aid the other should they be affected by a disaster.)

Attach any Memorandums or Letters of Understanding to the back of the plan.

1. Name of agency   *Contact information*

Service provided

2. Name of agency   *Contact information*

Service provided

3. Name of agency   *Contact information*

Service provided

4. Name of agency   *Contact information*

Service provided

Key Contacts

Accountant	*Telephone number*
Attorney	*Telephone number*
Bank	*Telephone number*
Billing/Invoicing Service	*Telephone number*
Benefits Administrator	*Telephone number*
Building Manager/Owner	*Telephone number*
Building Security	*Telephone number*
Creditor	*Telephone number*
Electric Company	*Telephone number*
Electrician	*Telephone number*
Email/Internet Service Provider	*Telephone number*
Emergency Management Agency	*Telephone number*
Fire Department	*Telephone number*
Gas Company	*Telephone number*
Generator Rental Company	*Telephone number*
Grocery Store (nearest one)	*Telephone number*
Hardware Store (nearest one)	*Telephone number*

Hazardous Materials	Telephone number
Hospital (nearest one)	Telephone number
Insurance Agent/Claims Reporting	Telephone number
IT/Computer Service Provider	Telephone number
Local Newspaper	Telephone number
Mental Health/Social Services Agency	Telephone number
Payroll Processing	Telephone number
Pharmacy (nearest one)	Telephone number
Plumber	Telephone number
Poison Control Center	Telephone number
Police Department (non-emergency)	Telephone number
Public Works Department	Telephone number
Telephone Company	Telephone number
Website Provider	Telephone number
Other	Telephone number

Evacuation Plan

INSTRUCTIONS: Complete each of the following items below to help your congregation learn how to plan and carry out evacuation procedures in the event of an emergency.

Evacuation Procedures

During church hours, everyone in the building will go to:

_____

Name of site

_____

Address

_____

City

_____

Name of site manager (if relocating to another business)   *Telephone number*

Directions to site:

_____

_____

_____

_____

Leader in charge at evacuation site:

_____

_____

_____

_____

Responsibilities include:

☐ Conducting attendance at site

☐ Bringing emergency documents and phone lists

☐ Bringing emergency kit

☐ Other:

Are there people who will need assistance evacuating your facility? If so, what assistance is needed?

_____

_____

Who will be responsible for the care of these individuals at the alternate site?

_____

_____

_____

_____

What will your members/visitors need that may not be available at a temporary location?

_____

_____

_____

_____

Transportation for moving members/visitors to a temporary location or to their homes will be provided by:

_____
Transportation company

_____
Contact name   *Telephone number*

_____
Alternate company

_____
Contact name   *Telephone number*

Evacuation Dos and Don'ts

Remain calm.

Follow the instructions of the incident coordinator or emergency response team, if applicable.

If you occupy an enclosed office, close the door as you leave.

Use stairwells (do not use elevator) for evacuation. Be alert for other staff, members and emergency agency personnel who might also be using the stairwells.

Do not return for coats, purses, briefcases, etc., after you have left the area.

Do not smoke.

Do not return to your area until the "all clear" signal is given.

Extended Relocation

If your current location is not accessible for an extended period of time, operations will be moved to the following location (attach Memorandum or Letter of Understanding to the back of this document):

_____

Name/owner

_____

Address

_____

City   *State*   *Zip*

_____

Telephone number   *Alternate number*

_____

Directions to relocation site:

_____

_____

_____

_____

Shelter in Place

INSTRUCTIONS: Complete the following items to plan ahead to ensure a safe and secure place for those who call your church their spiritual home, as well as community members who might seek refuge.

Shelter Considerations

If a "shelter in place" emergency is issued, we will move to the following room:

_____

_____

_____

_____

Ensure the following:

- ☐ All doors and windows are closed.
- ☐ Cracks around doors and windows are sealed with duct tape or plastic sheeting.
- ☐ All vents are closed and sealed.
- ☐ Any ventilation systems, motors or fans are turned off.
- ☐ Emergency supply kit is available.
- ☐ Listen to radio/television and follow directions from authorities until they issue an "all clear."

Church Go-Kit: Emergency Supplies Kit

INSTRUCTIONS: Check off common items needed for developing a Church Go-Kit. Items in an emergency supply kit may include but are not limited to the items listed below. Adjust these items to meet the needs of your congregation.

Supply Checklist

☐ Bible, hymnal, prayer book and/or other important items needed to carry out ministry

☐ Batteries—extra ones for flashlights and radios

☐ Blankets/sleeping bags/Mylar "space blankets"

☐ Bottled water (one gallon per person per day)

☐ Can opener (manual)

☐ Cash in small denominations (include correct change for pay phones)

☐ Duct tape

☐ Fire extinguisher

☐ First-aid kit (scissors, tweezers, Band-Aids, cotton balls, gauze pads/roller gauze and tape, antibacterial wipes, first-aid ointment, vinyl gloves, non-aspirin pain reliever, safety pins, first-aid book)

☐ Flashlight/light sticks

☐ Food/snacks (ready-to-eat canned goods, raisins, granola bars, etc.)

☐ Gloves

☐ Hand sanitizer

☐ NOAA weather alert radio

☐ Office supplies (notepads, pens)

☐ Paper plates, cups, utensils

☐ Paper towels, wipes

☐ Personal hygiene items

☐ Plastic bags—all sizes resealable bags and garbage bags

☐ Plastic sheeting

☐ Radio—battery operated

☐ Rope

☐ Tool kit (pliers, screwdriver, hammer, nails, crowbar, adjustable wrench, etc.)

☐ Change of clothes

☐ Whistle

☐ Other:

☐ Other:

Injury/Incident Report

INSTRUCTIONS: Complete this form should an injury occur during an evacuation or other emergency procedure. It is important to maintain accurate records of any injuries incurred during an emergency. This record can help injured individuals to gain better access to treatments, as well as help with potential insurance or liability questions.

Injury/Incident Report Form

Date: _____

Injured person: _____

Completed by: _____

Where were you when injury occurred?: _____

Description of injury and how it occurred: (Use back if more space is needed.)

_____

_____

_____

_____

_____

_____

_____

Witnesses:

Action taken/Medical treatment provided:

_____

_____

_____

_____

_____

_____

Training and Exercises

INSTRUCTIONS: Complete the following form to help your congregation and partners develop training and education strategies that will help put your plans into action.

Training Exercise Evaluation Form

Date and time of drill/exercise:

Type of drill/exercise:

Objectives of drill/exercise: (Objectives should be measurable.)

_____

_____

_____

_____

_____

_____

_____

_____

Staff participating:

_____

_____

_____

_____

_____

_____

_____

Assessment

Explain what worked well:

_____

_____

_____

_____

Explain what needs improvement/corrective action:

_____

_____

_____

_____

_____

_____

_____

Plan for improvement/corrective action:

_____

_____

_____

_____

_____

_____

Planned retest date:

_____

Evaluation completed by:

_____

Congregants with Disaster-Related Skills/Certifications/Resources

Sample Database of Congregants with Special Skills

Congregant's Name	Skill(s)
(Example) Julius Holleran	*Emergency room surgeon/Spanish*
(Example) Linda Barbaro	*Pastoral care skills*
(Example) David Hamilton	*Owner of moving business and vans*

Sample Disaster-Related Skill Questionnaire

Instructions: Distribute this questionnaire to congregants, then have them return the completed forms to the Disaster Leadership Team.

Basic Information

Date:	
Name:	
Address:	
Phones:	Home:
	Office:
	Cell:
Email:	

Special Skills I Would Volunteer

(Note: Any volunteer contact with youth requires Safe Church training.)

Yes/No	Skill	For Congregants	For Wider Community
	Language (which one):	Y / N	Y / N
	Evacuation	Y / N	Y / N
	Cleanup	Y / N	Y / N
	Emergency babysitting at home (how many children):	Y / N	Y / N
	Emergency babysitting at church/shelter (how many children):	Y / N	Y / N
	Transportation to doctor (how many people):	Y / N	Y / N
	Provide vehicle for evacuation or cleanup	Y / N	Y / N
	Provide boat for evacuation or cleanup	Y / N	Y / N
	Provide aircraft for evacuation or cleanup	Y / N	Y / N
	Provide portable generator	Y / N	Y / N
	Temporary housing (how many people):	Y / N	Y / N
	Provide nonperishable food	Y / N	Y / N
	Provide bottled water	Y / N	Y / N
	Provide hot meals or a covered dish	Y / N	Y / N
	Cook/serve meals	Y / N	Y / N
	Pray with/for victims	Y / N	Y / N
	Have first-aid/CPR certification	Y / N	Y / N
	Blood donation	Y / N	Y / N
	Other:	Y / N	Y / N

Professional Services

Yes/No	Professional Service	For Congregants	For Wider Community
	Medical assistance (nurse, MD, EMT, etc.)	Y / N	Y / N
	Legal assistance	Y / N	Y / N

Yes/No	Professional Service	For Congregants	For Wider Community
	Counseling assistance (LSW, LPC, etc.)	Y / N	Y / N
	Certified chaplain	Y / N	Y / N
	Ham radio operator	Y / N	Y / N
	Professional rebuilding assistance	Y / N	Y / N
	Professional tree services and removal	Y / N	Y / N
	Other:	Y / N	Y / N

Other Skills or Resources:

Yes/No	Skills/Resources	Description/Date	Willing to work outside congregation?
	Other disaster training (CERT, ARC, UMCARE)		Y / N
	Case management		Y / N
	Other: (project development, tools available list, other services, etc.)		Y / N

Return this form to:

Plan Implementation Procedures

INSTRUCTIONS: Use the information you have already provided to document what should happen after a disaster. The goal is to outline an action plan for who will do what following a disaster.

Sample Action Steps

First 10 steps:

	Step	Time Frame	Person Responsible
1	Notify church staff and elders (xxx-xxx-xxxx)		
2	Call Disaster Ministry Team to activate phone tree		
3	Call "sister" church at xxx-xxx-xxxx to inform them of evacuation and when they can expect evacuees		
4	Protect windows and doors, cover organ and unplug electronics		
5	Walk through church to make sure all valuables are stowed, protected or removed		
6	Take Church Go-Kit		
7	Activate evacuation plan for handicapped congregants		
8	Evacuate to "sister" church		
9	Activate phone tree/communication plans to check on safety of elderly members		
10	Provide congregation members updates through email list and church social media		

Part Five

Disaster Spiritual and Emotional Care Tip Sheets

Recognizing Common Disaster Survivor Stress Reactions

Aim	To be able to recognize common psychological and emotional, cognitive, behavioral, physical, and spiritual stress reactions.
General Information	Most people are resilient and experience mild or transient psychological disturbances from which they readily bounce back. The stress response becomes problematic when it does not or cannot turn off; that is, when symptoms last too long or interfere with daily life. The following provides a list of common stress reactions.
Psychological and Emotional	Feeling heroic, invulnerable, euphoric Denial Anxiety and fear Worry about safety of self and others Anger Irritability Restlessness Sadness, grief, depression, moodiness Distressing dreams Guilt or "survivor guilt" Feeling overwhelmed, hopeless Feeling isolated, lost or abandoned Apathy
Cognitive	Memory problems Disorientation Confusion Slowness of thinking and comprehension Difficulty calculating, setting priorities, making decisions Poor concentration Limited attention span Loss of objectivity Unable to stop thinking about the disaster Blaming
Behavioral	Change in activity Decreased efficiency and effectiveness Difficulty communicating Increased sense of humor Outbursts of anger, frequent arguments Inability to rest or "let down" Change in eating habits Change in sleeping patterns Change in patterns of intimacy, sexuality Change in job performance Periods of crying Increased use of alcohol, tobacco or drugs Social withdrawal, silence Vigilance about safety or environment Avoidance of activities or places that trigger memories Proneness to accidents
Physical	Increased heartbeat, respiration Increased blood pressure Upset stomach, nausea, diarrhea Change in appetite, weight loss or gain Sweating or chills Tremors (hands, lips) Muscle twitching "Muffled" hearing Tunnel vision Feeling uncoordinated Headaches Soreness in muscles Lower back pain Feeling a "lump in the throat" Exaggerated startle reaction Fatigue Menstrual cycle changes Change in sexual desire Decreased resistance to infection Flare-up of allergies and arthritis Hair loss
Spiritual	Questions about faith Self-blame Questioning God Anger at God Realization of mortality Withdrawal from faith and religion Concern about hereafter Questions about good and evil Questions about forgiveness Redefining moral values and intangible priorities Promising, bargaining with and challenging God Concern about vengeance Distressed by belief that deceased is separated from God Connection to faith is shaken Feels life has no meaning Stops relying on faith/prayer

Adapted from B. N. Goff and V. Hull, *Kansas All-Hazards Behavioral Health Program* (Topeka, KS: Kansas Department of Social and Rehabilitation Services, 2006).

Disaster Spiritual and Emotional Care Listening and Attending Skills

Aim	Disaster settings are normally chaotic, noisy and lacking privacy. As a result of reading this tip sheet, the designated emotional and spiritual caregiver can learn effective ways to create an environment that mitigates the effect of present distractions and stressors experienced by the individual, allowing him or her to process the experience of the disaster.
General Information	The goal is to use attentive listening skills in order to help the survivor understand his/her experience of the disaster, to feel heard and understood, and begin to feel some sense of control and relief as a result of the process.
	It is important to note that:
	Listening is an active process and not simply quietly taking in what someone is saying.
	It is not up to you to fix the situation. Instead, listen for the person's strengths, point them out, and suggest additional supports and resources as needed.
	Maintain an attitude of patience, calm and concern.
Create a Ministry of Presence	In emotional and spiritual care, emphasis is placed on being present with people. This is often referred to as the "ministry of presence."
	This ministry is to be fully with another person, exhibiting a nonanxious, comfortable presence while demonstrating "God with us" through the interconnectedness of the human interaction. It is the art of being with another.
	Elements of ministry of presence:
	"Showing up";
	"Being" rather than "doing";
	"Listening" rather than "talking";
	Meeting the survivor where they are at emotionally/psychologically;
	Demonstrating divine silence in which love rests secure;
	Giving a calm, accepting presence;
	Walking through the pain with another; and
	Living out the gospel through loving companionship (doesn't necessarily mean speaking about spiritual topics).
Key Attending Skills	There are three parts to active listening in a crisis: the setting, hearing the story and responding accurately and with care and respect.
	About the setting:
	Minimize distractions in the environment; this can be accomplished by relocating or positioning the individual's back to distractions.
	Be observant about the conditions and the survivor's appearance. Is the setting safe? Is it private? Does the survivor look like he or she feels safe? Does the survivor have obvious physical needs that you should discuss?
	Hear the story:
	Be fully present with the survivor; it is your job to set aside other thoughts and direct your attention to the survivor and what he or she is saying.
	Maintain a comfortable gaze; do not allow the eyes to shift, look around the room or take on an out-of-focus look.

Key Attending Skills (continued)	Maintain an engaged but unobtrusive body position. Three such body positions are: direct (face-to-face) body orientation, an angled body orientation and a side-by-side orientation. It has been noted that, on average, women are more likely to prefer the direct body orientation, while men tend to prefer the latter two body orientations. You will need to decide which orientation to use based on your assessment of the situation.
	Remember the importance of nonverbal messages. A lack of facial responsiveness or negative responses can quickly destroy a communication of interaction.
	Allow survivors to relate their experience of the disaster as they experienced it; this is often a necessary step that allows survivors to ground themselves in reality and make their felt pain real by linking it directly to their circumstance. The act of sharing can help validate the survivor's experience and aid the creation of a bond between survivor and caregiver.
	Respond with care and respect:
	Utilize empathy in the listening process; empathy is feeling and thinking with another person. If you are new to this, consider using a simple model, such as "When *(an event they shared with you)* occurred, then you felt *(their experience)."*
	It is okay if your reply misses the mark. The speaker usually will correct you, and then you can respond more accurately. You do not have to be accurate every time.
	As you start, keep your statements short and encourage the survivor to do most of the talking. Focus on helping them to tell their story. As their story is complete, then shift to asking about other aspects of the story and how they are coping.
	Remember this is not therapy; it is the job of the caregiver to recognize and redirect downward emotional spiraling, should it begin to occur.
What Not to Do	Don't problem solve too early; it is easy for caregivers to respond cognitively, thereby causing them to miss reinforcing what the survivor is saying. Instead, the caregiver must first allow the survivor to give voice to their situation and receive confirmation by the caregiver as to what they have said.
	Do not challenge, interpret or make statements about larger issues beyond the crisis. Your role is to reinforce strengths and add to them as needed.
	Don't interrupt the survivor too early with guiding questions; this may distract the thought process of the survivor and deter them from saying what needs to be said.

How *Not* to Provide Volunteer and Survivor Care

Aim	There are common statements that people make in everyday situations that can be harmful in a crisis situation. In this sheet we highlight these statements and provide ways to prevent them.
General Information	When providing support, you should avoid saying the following phrases. On the surface, these phrases may be meant to comfort volunteers or survivors, but they can be misinterpreted.
Basic Statements to Avoid	In general, well-intentioned statements that say to a person that their experience is not as bad as they think it is, or that oversimplify or minimize the experience, risk alienating, offending or even compounding the distress.
	"I understand." In most situations we cannot understand unless we have had the same experience.
	"Don't feel bad." The person has a right to feel bad and will need time to feel differently.
	"You're strong" or "You'll get through this." After a disaster, many people do not feel strong and question if they will recover from the loss.
	"Don't cry." It is okay to cry.
	"It's God's will." With a person you do not know, giving religious meaning to an event may insult or anger the person.
	"It could be worse," "At least you still have . . ." or "Everything will be okay." It is up to the individual to decide whether things could be worse or if everything can be okay.
	Rather than provide comfort, these types of responses could elicit a strong negative response or distance the individual from the listener. It is okay to apologize if the person reacts negatively to something that was said.
How to Avoid These Errors	You can learn to avoid these misstatements. If you are new to helping people in a crisis situation, then practice with someone by role-playing. Ask a friend or team member to play the part of someone who has just come through a crisis, and talk with them as though you are a counselor. This will help you build confidence that you can help and reduce the stress that leads to mistakes.
	Misstatements are more likely to happen when you are under stress, anxious to fix the situation or uncomfortable with the other person. Monitor your own stress and patience, and if you cannot listen patiently, take a break.
	Misstatements are more likely when we are unsure of what to say, and so fall back on quick or simplistic answers. Identify the situations most challenging for you and in which you are least sure of what to say, and practice responding with a friend or colleague.
	When you first start providing support to others in crisis, partner with someone who can listen to your conversations and then talk with you afterward about your approach, manner and ways to improve.

How to Avoid These Errors (continued)	Remember, it is okay to say you do not know or are unsure of what to say. Honesty is always a better course than trying to fix something you cannot fix or trying to have an answer for everything.
	Keep an open mind to learning. We are all students, and no matter your level of experience, everyone can learn ways to improve.
Action Steps for Clergy and Chaplains	As clergy or chaplain, you can help prepare people in ways that reduce the risk of errors.
	As you coach your volunteers, be careful about putting inexperienced people into difficult situations alone. Instead, put people into teams or pairs where new people can be coached and mentored by more experienced people.
	When you hold team meetings, ask people about difficult conversations they have had and role-play how to handle them.
	Encourage learning by being open about ways you also need to learn. Encourage people to also coach you and help you develop your skills. This openness makes it safer for people to be open about ways they need assistance.

Helping Volunteers Talk About Stress

Aim	The ability to talk about stress is basic to getting and providing support. This tip sheet highlights some of the topics of conversation and ways to start a conversation about them.
General Information	In a disaster situation, leaders likely will have volunteers who face highly stressful situations. Leaders can help volunteers limit the impact of stress in their lives by processing the experiences they have undergone. The following are some areas of potential concern that team leaders may consider talking with their volunteers about: Alcohol and substance abuse Anger problems Burnout Crosscultural issues Domestic violence Education problems Experiences during disaster relief/recovery Feelings of depression or anxiety Financial problems Grief management Health problems (headaches, heart palpitations, not taking care of oneself, etc.) Legal problems Limits and liabilities Medical conditions Mental health problems Relationship issues Risky behavior (fighting, speeding, etc.) Sleep problems/nightmares Talk of suicide
Sample Questions for Starting Dialogue	It takes practice to use questions so they are more of a conversation than an interview. An interview can feel too formal and actually lead a person to talk less as they expect you to ask all the questions. In order to be less formal, change the suggested questions so they are more consistent with your own style and relationship with the person you are speaking with. As you ask questions, listen for signs of concern, such as the person talking about any especially stressful experience. When you hear this, then gently prompt the person to tell you more. Focus on helping them to tell their story rather than interviewing them. What has happened since you've been in the field? How have you been spending your time? What is a typical day like? What kind of work are you doing? What are you doing to take care of yourself? How is that going?
Action Steps for Clergy and Chaplains	You have a role in setting expectations for the church or team. Therefore, you can establish expectations about sharing stress and being open about the experience of helping. In a culture where people may be slow to "unburden" themselves, you may have to clearly and repeatedly explain the importance of openness. Make it clear to your team and volunteers that talking about stress is essential, not optional, if they are going to thrive in this work.

Action Steps for Clergy and Chaplains (continued)	Make sure that your church and team provide an environment that is safe for talking openly by demonstrating respect, concern and support.
	Volunteers can mistakenly believe that if they show signs of distress then something is wrong with them, or they are weak, or they are less capable than others. Getting people to be open with one another about signs of stress is the most effective way to dispel these fears.
	Although most people will cope with their service to others in crisis, some people can become overwhelmed. Pastors and leaders must be prepared to counsel the struggling few that they may need to find other ways to serve.
When Talking Is Enough	Talking about a distressing experience is more than simple reporting. When people talk about an experience they are organizing and understanding the experience. They are also watching to see if what they share can be understood and if others have had a similar experience. This is called "normalizing," and it helps people to feel that their experience is manageable, and thus they feel more in control of what happened to them. In some cases people may need to do this several times until they begin to feel less distress.
When Talking Is *Not* Enough	In some cases the distress a person is experiencing is more complicated and their reaction to the distress is not easily managed. In these cases a person may be referred to a mental health professional who can recognize these complications and provide assistance.

How to Refer Disaster Survivors for Mental Health Care

Aim	It is important to remember that some disaster survivors may need additional follow-up services from a licensed mental health professional. Similarly, some relief workers and volunteers may also need additional assistance after particularly traumatic events. This tip sheet will help you know when and how to refer others for mental health care.
Signs That Suggest Help Is Needed	A more serious level of disturbance is seen in more severe symptoms, symptoms that persist more than a few days or symptoms that appear much later. Sometimes people begin to have unpredictable or extreme emotional reactions, engage in impulsive or risky behavior that is unlike them or resort to self-medication such as with drugs or alcohol. Such signs for concern include the following: Disorientation or confusion, and difficulty communicating thoughts Difficulty remembering instructions Difficulty maintaining balance Becoming easily frustrated and being uncharacteristically argumentative Inability to engage in problem solving and difficulty making decisions Unnecessary risk taking Tremors, headaches and nausea Unusual clumsiness Tunnel vision and muffled hearing Colds or flu-like symptoms Limited attention span and difficulty concentrating Loss of objectivity Inability to relax Refusal to follow orders or to leave the scene Increased use of drugs or alcohol
When to Refer	Do not hesitate to admit that you don't know how to solve the problem, or if additional care is needed. Just be willing to help the person find someone who might know or has additional training. As you make the referral, remind disaster survivors that you do care. You care enough to want the best possible help or service for that person. Next are examples of when to refer: You feel in over your head. You feel persistently uncomfortable. You believe that improvement is "impossible" or the situation is "hopeless." The person you visit with says, "Nothing is helping," or what you provide the person isn't helping. There is an obvious change in speech and/or appearance. The person continues to be so emotional he or she can't communicate. There is ongoing deterioration of life (social and physical). All the person discusses are physical complaints. There is a sudden onset of memory confusion. You see signs/know of substance abuse.

When to Refer (continued)	The person has hallucinations, delusions or severe pathology.
	You observe threats of self-harm or harm to others.
	The person displays aggression and abuse (verbal and physical).
	The situation seems horrible or unbearable.
	Most importantly, if you're unsure, then refer.
How to Refer	Protect privacy—find private space and try to avoid interruptions while you are talking. Sensitivity to disaster survivors' privacy communicates trust, respect and sincerity.
	Discuss specific behaviors—prior to discussing the referral, list the behaviors you've seen exhibited that have raised concern. Your list might include withdrawal, anger, self-destructive action, depression, lack of sleep or loss of appetite.
	Ask what the disaster survivor thinks and feels—check for understanding, and support any attempts disaster survivors make to respond to the concerns you've voiced.
	Understand possible barriers and offer alternatives—before you approach disaster survivors about the problems, understand what barriers may be keeping him or her from seeking professional help and be able to offer suggestions to help overcome these barriers.
	Locate possible community resources—before talking with disaster survivors, you also need to know what community resources are available. Making the first contact often is the most difficult part of getting help. It can be helpful to provide a list of resources and licensed mental health professionals.
	Continue to be supportive—no matter how much you prepare disaster survivors, you still may not be able to convince them to seek professional help.
	Making independent referrals—if the person or family is unwilling to make the contact or if there is some danger if action is not taken, to self or others, you should take immediate action and begin the process for an independent referral and help obtain additional care. Remember, in such situations, serious concerns about harm to self or others should not be kept confidential.

Recognizing and Preventing Burnout in Yourself

Aim	This tip sheet provides guidance on recognizing when you are at risk of burning out, or starting to burn out, and what to do when you see the key signs.
General Information	Burnout is a state of emotional, physical and spiritual exhaustion from prolonged stress. When you are in a situation where the demands exceed your resources and it continues for a long time, then you are at significant risk of burnout.
	It is important to recognize, prevent and treat burnout because it destroys your productivity, saps your energy and, in extreme cases, can lead to a total collapse. This starts with understanding the difference between stress and burnout. Stress is a state of *activation*. We face challenges or threats and our bodies activate for action. Signs of stress include:
	Anxiety
	Sleeplessness
	Pressure
	A sense that life would be okay if you just got things under control
	Burnout comes from prolonged stress and is a state of *deactivation* that includes:
	Withdrawal
	Depression
	Feeling hopeless
	Discouragement about life
Ways You May Be At Risk	There are many factors that put us at risk of burnout, including personal, social and work-related factors.
	Personal factors include being a perfectionist or demanding near perfection from self and/or others; being pessimistic or negative, quick to find fault; feeling the need to personally be in control of everything around you; multiple physical ailments; and being a Type A personality with great demands for achievement. You can see that these personal factors increase stress and make it difficult to relieve constant stress.
	Social factors include unresolved marital or family problems, many people with expectations for you to help them, lack of friendships or close relationships, insufficient sleep, lack of exercise, or feeling that you have many demands with little help or support from others.
	Work factors include working extended periods of time without a break, unclear or poorly defined expectations, a sense of failure or fear of losing your job, working in a disorganized or chaotic environment, or working with little or no recognition or support.
	You may see that these signs can describe the life of many other helpers.
Signs You Are Experiencing Burnout	There are multiple signs of burnout in addition to the few mentioned above. They can be grouped as physical, emotional, behavioral and spiritual signs.
	Physical signs of burnout include:
	Chronic fatigue
	Low energy
	Low immunity; frequently ill
	Poor or changing appetite

Signs You Are Experiencing Burnout (continued)	Emotional signs include:
	    Self-doubt or a sense of failure
	    Constant self-doubt or questioning
	    Flat affect, lack of enjoyment in things that usually make you happy
	    Sense of defeat and discouragement
	
	Behavioral signs of burnout include:
	    Procrastination or avoidance of responsibility
	    Withdrawal or isolation of yourself from others
	    Turning to excess food or drugs
	    Lack of discipline in your self-care, such as exercise, hygiene or grooming
	
	Spiritual signs of burnout include:
	    Spiritual disconnection and isolation (e.g., "God has abandoned me.")
	    Religious strain (e.g., "God is so far away from me.")
	    Major changes in spiritual meaning-making (e.g., "Why would a good God let such a bad thing happen—I don't think I can believe in that God anymore.")

What to Do About Burnout	You address burnout with the three *R*s: Recognition, Reversal and Resilience
	
	Recognition—Learn the warning signs of burnout (above). Ask yourself if you are someone who tends to ignore your personal needs. If the answer is "yes," then ask someone who knows you and whom you trust to watch you for signs of burnout.
	
	Reversal—When you see the signs of burnout, then start to reverse the burnout by making rest, care and lowered stress a high priority. That does not mean you have to stop everything you are doing. It does mean that no one can function at a state of high stress without a break. Take these steps:
	    Lower the demands on yourself, at least temporarily. In the long term you will accomplish more if you vary the demands and stress.
	    Emphasize tasks within your control. Feeling out of control is distressing. If your work places demands that you cannot fulfill, then you must renegotiate them.
	    Build in a regular time when you are away from the demands.
	    Take up alternate activities that are satisfying and low stress.
	    We all have multiple areas of our life, such as marriage, family life, career, social life, etc. Make it a priority to ensure that you do not face great stress in more than one area at a time. If there are problems in marriage or family as well as work, then deal with the personal areas of your life first and lower the conflict or stress.
	
	Resilience—Examine your lifestyle and look for ways to build your ability to withstand stress. Participate in activities that provide rest and improve your self-management. Seek out spiritual and social support.

Strategies for Self-Care

Aim	This sheet explains the importance of intentionally taking care of oneself (meaning actively and with specific strategies) in stressful situations. Equipping staff with the skills of self-care, and clergy and chaplains modeling self-care, will reduce the risk of unhealthy effects from stress.
General Information	An important factor in the health of any organization is the vitality of its members. By acting intentionally in promoting good habits of self-care, the church can protect its members from the harmful effects of stress. Here are tips that will help you get started.
Plan Well	Set a goal and break it down into easily managed pieces. This helps staff to see they are making progress and reduces the stress of possibly overwhelming aims. Take small steps, working through each piece, until you reach your goal. Reward yourself as you complete each step and when you reach the goal. (A reward can be a break, some social time or just working on a less demanding task.) Tell others in your life what your goals are and enlist their support. After you reach your goal, work to maintain your improvements.
Maintain Faith	Get in touch with and do things you find uplifting, noble or creative. Read spiritual, inspirational or religious materials, such as Scripture. Get involved in a religious community and discuss spiritual topics with others. Attend religious ceremonies and engage in religious rituals like prayer, meditation, listening to religious music and observing religious symbols. If you have had bad experiences with religion or spirituality in the past, talk to someone you trust, such as a close friend, chaplain or counselor.
Balance Life Activities	Engage in meaningful leisure activities, including activities you have enjoyed in the past and new activities that get you out of a weekly pattern. Schedule regular vacations and be intentional in finding times to relax. Exercise regularly—twenty to thirty minutes three or four times a week. Sleep is important. Try to go to bed and wake up the same time each day. Eat three balanced meals each day. Breakfast is especially important.
Keep an Optimistic Perspective	Balance the aspects of situations—avoid focusing only on the negative. Recognize that there are multiple contributing factors to your difficulties. Focus on the big picture and avoid all-or-nothing thinking. Think realistically and gather the facts—avoid jumping to conclusions. Avoid rigid expectations; watch for the words *should*, *must* or *have to* in your speech and thoughts.

Action Steps for Clergy and Chaplains	Clergy and chaplains are role models for their staff and volunteers. Set a good example by clearly demonstrating the skills of self-care.
	Teach the skills to your staff and team. It is easy to assume everyone knows how to do this, but it is often not true.
	Start with recognizing the need for self-care.
	Describe the impacts of stress and encourage awareness of those signs.
	Set an example by being open about stress.

Acknowledgments

We would like to thank our editor, Al Hsu, for all his guidance and support throughout the publishing process. We would also like to acknowledge and thank our very talented doctoral students Alice Schruba and Marianne Millen for helping pull together resources and research for this book. Thanks also to Linda Bretz, former HDI coordinator, for her help formatting and organizing the resources and tools for the book.

Thanks go out as well to all the other great students in our HDI lab who are making a difference in the lives of those impacted by disasters. We are grateful for all of our collaborators, including colleagues at Wheaton College and beyond. Our gratitude also goes out to all the churches, organizations and communities that have given us the privilege to walk alongside them and learn from them as they faced and overcame disaster.

Our thanks also go out to the John Templeton Foundation for their generous support of our research on faith and disaster issues. This book was made possible through the support of a grant from the John Templeton Foundation (Grant #44040). The opinions expressed in this publication are those of the authors and do not necessarily reflect the views of the John Templeton Foundation.

Notes

1 Introduction

[1]D. Guha-Sapir, F. Vos, R. Below and S. Ponserre, *Annual Disaster Statistical Review 2010* (Brussels: Centre for Research on the Epidemiology of Disasters, 2011).

[2]"Background Report: 9/11, Ten Years Later," START, 2011, www.start.umd.edu/sites/default/files/files/announcements/BackgroundReport_10YearsSince9_11.pdf.

[3]Humanitarian Disaster Institute, *Ready Faith: Planning Guide* (Wheaton, IL: Humanitarian Disaster Institute, 2013), 4, www.wheaton.edu/HDI/~/media/Files/Centers-and-Institutes/HDI/RF-Planning%20 Guide.pdf.

[4]J. D. Aten, R. A. Gonzalez, D. M. Boan, S. Topping, W. V. Livingston and J. M. Hosey, "Church Attendee Help Seeking Priorities After Hurricane Katrina in Mississippi and Louisiana: A Brief Report," *International Journal of Emergency Mental Health* 14, no. 1 (2011): 15-20.

[5]B. L. Whittington and S. J. Scher, "Prayer and Subjective Well-Being: An Examination of Six Different Types of Prayer," *International Journal for the Psychology of Religion* 20, no. 1 (2010): 59-68.

[6]H. Koenig, *In the Wake of Disaster: Religious Responses to Terrorism and Catastrophe* (Philadelphia: Templeton Foundation Press, 2006).

[7]US Department of Education, *Practical Information on Crisis Planning: A Guide for Schools and Communities* (Washington, DC: US Department of Education, 2003), 1-1.

[8]Church World Service Emergency Response Program, *Prepare to Care: Basic Disaster Ministry for Your Congregation*, 10th ed. (New York: Church World Service, 2009).

[9]K. Trader-Leigh, *Understanding the Role of African American Churches and Clergy in Community Crisis Response* (Washington, DC: Joint Center for Political and Economic Studies Health Policy Institute, 2009).

[10]See, for example, ready.gov and United Methodist Committee on Relief, *Connecting Neighbors: Organizing the Local Church for Disaster Ministry* (Washington, DC: UMCOR, 2010).

[11]See FEMA, *Guide for Developing High-Quality Emergency Operation Plans for Houses of Worship* (Washington, DC: FEMA, 2013); Church World Service Emergency Response Program, *Prepare to Care: Basic Disaster Ministry for Your Congregation*, 10th ed. (New York: Church World Service, 2009); Episcopal Relief & Development. *Preparedness and Planning Guide for Congregations and Parishes (Comprehensive Version)* (New York, NY: 2011); and Convoy of Hope, *H.O.P.E. Begins Here: Helping Others Prepared for Emergencies*, http://hopebeginshere.org.

2 Disaster Basics

[1]S. Jain, L. Kamimoto, A. M. Bramley, A. M. Schmitz, S. R. Benoit, J. Louie and L. Finelli, "Hospitalized Patients with 2009 H1N1 Influenza in the United States, April–June 2009," *New England Journal of Medicine* 361, no. 20 (2009): 1935-44.

[2]"H1N1 Flu," Centers for Disease Control and Prevention, last modified February 10, 2010, www.cdc.gov/h1n1flu/qa.htm.

[3]Lutheran Disaster Response, *Congregational Disaster Preparedness Guidebook* (Chicago: Evangelical Lutheran Church in America, 2014).

[4]Oklahoma Medical Reserve Corps, "Defining a Disaster," www.okmrc.org/disaster/define.cfm. See the article for more information about the characteristics of disasters.

[5]"Natural Disasters," Department of Homeland Security, last modified December 18, 2013, www.ready.gov/natural-disasters.

[6]Humanitarian Disaster Institute, *Ready Faith: Planning Guide* (Wheaton, IL: Humanitarian Disaster Institute, 2013), www.wheaton.edu/HDI/~/media/Files/Centers-and-Institutes/HDI/RF-Planning%20Guide.pdf.

[7]"Bioterrorism and Your Family: Manmade and Technological Threats," Center for Food Security and Public Health, January 1, 2010, accessed September 15, 2014, www.prep4agthreats.org/Assets/Factsheets/Bioterrorism-and-Your-Family.pdf.

[8]"H1N1 Flu."

[9]The more common number of 36,000 deaths per year was published in 1999 and may be too high. As a result CDC now prefers to state a range depending on the virus strain. "Estimating Seasonal Influenza-Associated Deaths in the United States: CDC Study Confirms Variability of Flu," Centers for Disease Control and Prevention, last modified September 12, 2013, www.cdc.gov/flu/about/disease/us_flu-related_deaths.htm.

[10]"CDC Estimates of Foodborne Illness in the United States," Centers for Disease Control, April 17, 2014, www.cdc.gov/foodborneburden/estimates-overview.html.

[11]US Department of Health and Human Services, Substance Abuse and Mental Health Services Administration, "Training Manual for Mental Health and Human Services Workers in Major Disasters," 2nd ed. (Washington, DC: 2000).

[12]Ibid.

[13]Ibid.

[14]Ibid.

[15]Nel and M. Righarts, "Natural Disasters and the Risk of Violent Civil Conflict," *International Studies Quarterly* 52, no. 1 (2008): 159-85.

[16]US Department of Health and Human Services, "Training Manual for Mental Health and Human Services Workers in Major Disasters."

[17]Ibid.

[18]Ibid.

[19]Humanitarian Disaster Institute, *Ready Faith: Planning Guide*.

[20]From https://em.countyofdane.com/mitigation_plan.aspx.

[21]Humanitarian Disaster Institute, *Ready Faith: Planning Guide*.

3 Disasters, Justice and the Church

[1]A. B. Cowey, "The Urban Coast from a National Perspective," *Coastal Management* 6, nos. 2-3 (1979): 135-65.

[2]O. D. Cardona, M. K. van Aalst, J. Birkmann, M. Fordham, G. McGregor, R. Perez, R. S. Pulwarty, E. L. F. Schipper and B. T. Sinh, "Determinants of Risk: Exposure and Vulnerability," in *Managing the Risks of Extreme Events and Disasters to Advance Climate Change Adaptation* (Cambridge: Cambridge University Press, 2012).

[3]United Nations, "Implementation of the International Strategy for Disaster Reduction," Report of the Secretary-General, August 12, 2011, www.unisdr.org/files/resolutions/A66301E.pdf.

[4]V. B. Davis, *Lost and Turned Out: A Guide to Preparing Underserved Communities for Disasters* (Vincent B. Davis, 2012).

[5]Thomas Pogge, *World Poverty and Human Rights* (Malden, MA: Polity Press, 2008).

[6]S. B. Manyena, "The Concept of Resilience Revisited, *Disasters* 30, no. 4 (2006): 434-50.

[7]Convoy of Hope, *Continuity of Ministry & Operations Plan (COMOP): Phase 1: Get Organized* (Springfield, MO: Convoy of Hope, 2009), 4.

[8]Humanitarian Disaster Institute, *Spiritual First Aid: Disaster Chaplain Guide* (Wheaton, IL: Humanitarian Disaster Institute, 2013).

[9]S. M. Southwick and D. S. Charney, *Resilience: The Science of Mastering Life's Greatest Challenges* (Cambridge: Cambridge University Press, 2012).

[10]Humanitarian Disaster Institute, *Spiritual First Aid: Disaster Chaplain Guide.*

[11]G. H. Brenner, D. H. Bush and J. Moses, eds. *Creating Spiritual and Psychological Resilience: Integrating Care in Disaster Relief Work* (New York: Routledge, 2010).

4 Getting Started

[1]Case study authors: Andrea Brim and Sandy Branda of First Presbyterian Church of Glen Ellyn, Illinois. I (David) am part of a small group that created and initiated a disaster ministry for our church. This account was written by two members of our group.

[2]K. M. Haueisen and C. Flores, *A Ready Hope: Effective Disaster Ministry for Congregations* (Lanham, MD: Rowman & Littlefield, 2009).

[3]Humanitarian Disaster Institute, *Public Health Planning Guide for Faith Communities* (Wheaton, IL: Humanitarian Disaster Institute, 2013).

[4]Convoy of Hope, *Continuity of Ministry & Operations Plan (COMOP): Phase 1: Get Organized* (Springfield, MO: Convoy of Hope, 2009), 6-7, 18. Convoy of Hope wisely recommends (1) getting senior leadership on board, (2) identifying a leader to head up the disaster ministry, (3) forming a team to prepare and help the church respond to disasters and (4) suggesting leaders keep in mind how important it is for them to serve as models to the congregation.

[5]The North Carolina Conference of the United Methodist Church, *A Disaster Response Plan for the North Carolina Conference* (2014).

[6]"Be Informed: Learn What Protective Measures to Take Before, During, and After an Emergency," Department of Homeland Security, last modified February 4, 2014, www.ready.gov/be-informed.

[7]Federal Emergency Management Agency, "Community Emergency Response Teams," www.fema.gov /community-emergency-response-teams.

[8]B. Rzengota, "The Changing Role of Churches in Disaster Relief and Management" (Master of Arts Integrated Research Project, Crown College, MN, 2014).

[9]Federal Emergency Management Agency (FEMA), *Voluntary Agency Liaison*, www.fema.gov/media -library-data/20130726-1829-25045-8002/val_brochure_final.pdf.

[10]See the National Voluntary Organizations Active in Disaster website, www.nvoad.org.

[11]See the American Red Cross website, www.redcross.org.

5 Planning

[1]J. Aten and S. Topping, "An Online Social Networking Disaster Preparedness Tool for Faith Communities," *Psychological Trauma: Theory, Research, Practice, and Policy* (2010): 2, 130-134.

[2]D. Sontag and R. Gebeloff, "The Downside of the Boom," *The New York Times* (Nov, 22, 2014), www .nytimes.com/interactive/2014/11/23/us/north-dakota-oil-boom-downside.html?_r=0.

[3]"Prepare for Disasters," World Renew, 2014, http://worldrenew.net/prepare-disasters.

[4]Centers for Disease Control and Prevention, *Public Health Workbook to Define, Locate, and Reach Special, Vulnerable, and At-Risk Populations in an Emergency* (Atlanta: CDC, 2010).

[5]Humanitarian Disaster Institute, *Ready Faith: Planning Guide* (Wheaton, IL: Humanitarian Disaster Institute, 2013), 4, www.wheaton.edu/HDI/~/media/Files/Centers-and-Institutes/HDI/RF-Planning%20 Guide.pdf.

[6]Humanitarian Disaster Institute, *Public Health Planning Guide for Faith Communities* (Wheaton, IL: Humanitarian Disaster Institute, 2013).

[7]Jamie Aten, Kari O'Grady, Glen Milstein, David Boan and Alice Schruba, "Spiritually Oriented Disaster Psychology," *Spirituality in Clinical Practice* 1 (2014): 20-28.

[8]S. L. Rasmussen, *Disaster Preparedness and Response in Province IV of the Episcopal Church* (Morganton, NC: Province IV of the Episcopal Church, 2009).

[9]K. M. Haueisen and C. Flores, *A Ready Hope: Effective Disaster Ministry for Congregations* (Lanham, MD: Rowman & Littlefield, 2009).

[10]See the Ready website, www.ready.gov.

6 Response

[1]Catherine McNiel, "Helping When Our Neighbors Are Hurting," *Life at Wheaton Bible Church* (Spring 2013), http://lifeatwheatonbiblechurch.com/2013/03/10/helping-when-our-neighbors-are-hurting. Used by permission.

[2]Hope Crisis Response Network, *Hope Crisis Response Network Disaster Planning for Churches* (Elkhart, IN: 2014).

[3]Humanitarian Disaster Institute, *Ready Faith: Planning Guide* (Wheaton, IL: Humanitarian Disaster Institute, 2013), www.wheaton.edu/HDI/~/media/Files/Centers-and-Institutes/HDI/RF-Planning%20 Guide.pdf.

[4]R. Setzke, *Crisis Communication Plan: Nonprofit Toolkit* (Denver: Colorado Nonprofit Association, 2006), www.coloradononprofits.org/wp-content/uploads/crisiscomm.pdf.

[5]GuideOne Center for Risk Management, *Safe Church: Emergency Action and Recovery Plan* (West Des Moines, IA: GuideOne, 2010).

[6]From FEMA, "IS-36 - Multihazard Planning for Childcare," Lesson 1: Course Overview, https://emilms .fema.gov/is36/MPCsummary.htm.

[7]Brotherhood Mutual Insurance Company, "Guidelines for Making Your Church a Temporary Shelter for Disaster Victims," www.brotherhoodmutual.com/index.cfm/resources/ministry-safety/article/guide lines-for-making-your-church-a-temporary-shelter-for-disaster-victims (accessed August 28, 2015).

[8]"Helping Others Prepare for Emergencies," Convoy of Hope, 2010, www.hopebeginshere.org.

[9]American Red Cross, *Fact Sheet on Shelter-in-Place*, February 2003, www.nationalterroralert.com /readyguide/shelterinplace.pdf.

[10]A number of these bullet points are drawn from Convoy of Hope, *Continuation of Ministry & Operations Plan, Phase One: Get Organized* (Springfield, MO: Convoy of Hope, 2009), http://hopebeginshere.org /go/church/entry/templates_and_resources, 22.

[11]K. Leavell, J. Aten and D. Boan, "The Lived Coping Experiences of South Mississippi and New Orleans Clergy Affected by Hurricane Katrina: An Exploratory Study," *Journal of Psychology & Theology* 40 (2012): 336-48.

[12]"Public and Community Safe Rooms," Federal Emergency Management Agency (FEMA), last modified July 24, 2014, www.fema.gov/safe-rooms/public-and-community-safe-rooms.

[13]Federal Emergency Management Agency (FEMA), *Community-Based Pre-Disaster Mitigation for Community and Faith-Based Organizations Instructor Guide* (Washington, DC: FEMA, 2004), 4.

[14]GuideOne, *Safe Church*.

7 Recovery

[1]Case study authors: Bruce Rzengota and Darin Mather of Crown College, St. Bonifacius, Minnesota.

[2]"Who We Are," National Voluntary Organizations Active in Disaster, 2014, www.nvoad.org/about-us.

[3]See the Christian Emergency Network website, www.christianemergencynetwork.org.

[4]See the National Disaster Interfaiths Network website for more information and a list of active networks, www.n-din.org.

[5]See the National Voluntary Organizations Active in Disaster website, www.nvoad.org.

[6]For more information about the Disaster Ministry Conference, visit wheaton.edu/HDI.

[7]Church World Service Emergency Response Program, *Prepare to Care: Guide to Disaster Ministry in Your Congregation*, 10th ed. (New York: Church World Service, 2009).

[8]"Faith Communities and Disasters," University of Southern California, accessed September 15, 2014, http://crcc.usc.edu/initiatives/fcd/resourcelist.html.

[9]J. Aten and S. Topping, "An Online Social Networking Disaster Preparedness Tool for Faith Communities," *Psychological Trauma: Theory, Research, Practice, and Policy* 2 (2010): 130-34; T. D. Stuart, G. M. McMillon and R. S. Chandler, "Faith Communities, FCS, and Natural Disasters: Expanding the Helping Network," *Journal of Family & Counseling Sciences* 102, no. 3 (Summer 2010): 41.

[10]"Community Arise: A Disaster Ministry Curriculum," Community Arise, 2012, www.communityarise .com.

[11]R. Bagley, *Group's Emergency Response Handbook for Disaster Relief* (Loveland, CO: Group Publishing, 2009); K. M. Haueisen and C. Flores, *A Ready Hope: Effective Disaster Ministry for Congregations* (Lanham, MD: Rowman & Littlefield, 2009); Church World Service Emergency Response Program, *Community Arise: A Disaster Ministry Curriculum* (New York: Church World Service, 2012), www.com munityarise.com; FEMA, *Developing and Managing Volunteers* (Washington, DC: FEMA, 2006); Points of Light Foundation & Volunteer Center National Network, *Managing Spontaneous Volunteers in Times of Disaster: The Synergy of Structure and Good Intentions* (Washington, DC: Points of Light, 2005); National Voluntary Organizations Active in Disaster, *Long Term Recovery Guide* (Alexandria, VA; National Voluntary Organizations in Disaster, 2012), 26-27.

[12]Humanitarian Disaster Institute, *Ready Faith: Planning Guide* (Wheaton, IL: Humanitarian Disaster Institute, 2013), www.wheaton.edu/HDI/~/media/Files/Centers-and-Institutes/HDI/RF-Planning%20 Guide.pdf.

[13]R. A. Karaban, *Crisis Caring: A Guide for Ministering to People in Crisis* (San Jose, CA: Resource Publications, 2005); J. Aten, K. O'Grady, G. Milstein, D. Boan and A. Schruba, "Spiritually Oriented Disaster Psychology," *Spirituality in Clinical Practice* 1, no. 1 (2014): 20-28.

[14]G. McCaskill, M. Parker, D. Boan and J. D. Aten, "Fatalities and Old Age: Reported Deaths from the Tuscaloosa Tornado" (poster presentation, Rural Health Institute, Birmingham, AL, April 2012).

[15]Church World Service, *A Capacity Building Guidebook: Managing & Operating A Disaster Long-Term Recovery Organization* (New York: Church World Service, 2009).

[16]National Volunteer Organizations Active in Disaster (NVOAD), *Long Term Recovery Guide*, 2012, www .nvoad.org/wp-content/uploads/2014/04/long_term_recovery_guide_-_final_2012.pdf.

[17]FEMA, *Disaster Case Management Program Guidance* (Washington, DC: Department of Homeland Security, 2013), www.fema.gov/media-library-data/20130726-1908-25045-2403/dcm_pg_ final_3_8_13.pdf.

[18]National Voluntary Organizations Active in Disasters, *When Disaster Strikes . . . How to Donate or Volunteer Successfully!* (Alexandria, VA: National Voluntary Organizations Active in Disasters, 2007); Church World Service Emergency Response Program, *Community Arise: A Disaster Ministry Curriculum* (New York: Church World Service, 2012), www.communityarise.com; California-Nevada Conference Disaster Response Ministry, *Local Church Disaster Planning Guide* (United Methodist Church, 2009); US Department of Homeland Security, *Target Capabilities List: A Companion to the National Preparedness Guidelines* (Washington, DC: US Department of Homeland Security, 2007).

[19]Don Philpott and Michael W. Kuenstle, "School Safety Planning and Preparedness," in *Education Facility Security Handbook* (Lanham, MD: Government Institutes, 2007).

[20]Jamie Aten, "How Churches Can Help Without Hurting After Super Typhoon Haiyan," *Christianity Today*, November 8, 2013, www.christianitytoday.com/ct/2013/november-web-only/how-to-help-after-super-typhoon-haiyan.html.

[21]Ibid.

[22]VT UCC Disaster Response Coordinators, *Planning Your Church Mission, Role and Response in Case of Emergency or Disaster* (Randolph, VT: United Church of Christ, 2008).

8 Providing Basic Disaster Spiritual and Emotional Care

[1]National Center for PTSD, *Mental Health Reactions After Disasters* (Washington, DC: US Department for Veterans Affairs, 2010); SAMHSA, *Tips for Survivors of a Disaster or Other Traumatic Events: Managing Stress* (Washington, DC: SAMHSA, 2013), HHS Publication No. SmA-13-4776.

[2]D. Burr, *Operation Blue Roof: Protocol on the Deployment of Americorps Teams for Disaster Recovery* (FL: Corporation for National & Community Service, n.d.), www.nationalservice.gov/resources/disaster-services/providing-emotional-support-volunteers-disaster-situations.

[3]N. Murray-Swank, "Seeking the Sacred: The Assessment of Spirituality in the Therapy Process," in *Spiritually Oriented Interventions for Counseling and Psychotherapy*, ed. K. I. Pargament, J. D. Aten, M. R. McMinn and E. L. Worthington (Washington, DC: American Psychological Association, 2011), 107-35; see also H. Koenig, *In the Wake of Disaster: Religious Responses to Terrorism and Catastrophe* (Philadelphia: Templeton Foundation Press, 2006); S. Roberts and W. Ashley, *Disaster Spiritual Care: Practical Clergy Responses to Community, Regional, and National Tragedy* (Woodstock, VT: SkyLight Paths Publishing, 2008).

[4]H. N. Wright, *The Complete Guide to Crisis and Trauma Counseling: What to Do and Say When It Matters Most!* (Ventura, CA: Regal, 2011); L. G. Calhoun and R. G. Tedeschi, *Posttraumatic Growth in Clinical Practice* (New York: Routledge, 2012).

[5]National Voluntary Organizations Active in Disasters, *Light Our Way: A Guide for Spiritual Care in Times of Disaster* (Alexandria, VA: National Voluntary Organizations Active in Disasters, 2006).

[6]See, e.g., H. N. Wright, *Crisis Counseling: What to Do and Say During the First 72 Hours* (Ventura, CA: Regal, 1993); Wright, *Crisis and Trauma Counseling*.

[7]K. L. Ellers, *Emotional and Spiritual Care in Disasters: Participant Guide* (International Critical Stress Foundation, 2008).

[8]Church World Service Emergency Response Program, *Community Arise: Emotional and Spiritual Care in Disasters (Participant Guide)* (New York: Church World Service, 2008), 66.

[9]Carol Hacker, *Too Much, Too Ugly, Too Fast! How Faith Communities Can Respond in Crisis and Disasters* (Chicago: Lutheran Disaster Response, 2003).

[10]J. Aten, K. O'Grady, G. Milstein, D. Boan and A. Schruba, "Spiritually Oriented Disaster Psychology," *Spirituality in Clinical Practice* 1, no. 1 (2014): 20-28.

[11]C. L. Parker, D. J. Barnett, G. S. Everly and J. M. Links, "Establishing Evidence-Informed Core Intervention Competencies in Psychological First Aid for Public Health Personnel," *International Journal of Emergency Mental Health* 8, no. 2 (2006): 83-92. G. S. Everly, "Thoughts on Early Intervention," *International Journal of Emergency Mental Health* 3, no. 4 (2001): 201-10.

[12]F. P. Buttell and M. M. Carney, "Examining the Impact of Hurricane Katrina on Police Responses to Domestic Violence," *Traumatology* 15, no. 2 (2009): 6-9.

[13]Wright, *Crisis and Trauma Counseling*.

[14]SAMHSA, *Tips for Talking With and Helping Children and Youth Cope After a Disaster or Traumatic Event: A Guide for Parents, Caregivers, and Teachers* (Rockville, MD: SAMHSA, 2013), HHS Publication No. SMA-12-4732.

[15]J. Shaw, Z. Espinel and J. Shultz, "Care of Children Exposed to the Traumatic Effects of Disaster" (Washington, DC: American Psychiatric Publishing, 2012).

[16]Barbara Couden Hernandez and Jamie D. Aten, "Children's Perceptions of God's Role in Their Families: An Exploratory Study," in *A Christian Worldview and Mental Health*, ed. Carlos Fayard, Barbara Couden Hernandez, Bruce Anderson and George T. Harding IV (Berrien Springs, MI: Andrews University Press).

[17]J. Crisp, *Ministering to Children After Disasters* (New York: Episcopal Relief & Development, 1999); J. Aten, D. Boan, K. Flanagan, S. Canning, S. Hall, E. Eveleigh, S. Rueger, E. Kang and J. Pressley, *Helping Children Cope with Traumatic Events* (Wheaton, IL: Humanitarian Disaster Institute, 2012), 5.

[18]Shaw et al., "Care of Children"; A. H. Speier, *Psychosocial Issues for Children and Adolescents in Disasters*, 2nd ed. (Rockville, MD: SAMHSA, 2005), DHHS Publication No. ADM 86-1070R; Church World Service, *Community Arise: Children, Youth and Disaster* (New York: Church World Service, 2006).

[19]SAMHSA, *Tips for Supervisors of Disaster Responders: Helping Staff Manage Stress When Returning to Work* (Rockville, MD: SAMHSA, 2014).

[20]Humanitarian Disaster Institute, "Tip Sheet: How to Refer Disaster Survivors for Mental Health Care" (Wheaton, IL: Humanitarian Disaster Institute, 2012), www.wheaton.edu/HDI/%7E/media/Files /Centers-and-Institutes/HDI/DSEC-HowtoReferDisasterSurvivorsforMentalHealthCare.pdf.

[21]J. D. Aten and D. Boan, *Spiritual First Aid: Disaster Chaplain Guide* (Wheaton, IL: Humanitarian Disaster Institute, 2013); W. P. Nash, R. J. Westphal, P. J. Watson and B. T. Litz, *Combat and Operational Stress First Aid: Caregiver Training Manual* (Washington, DC: US Navy, Bureau of Medicine and Surgery, 2010); National Disaster Interfaiths Network, "Tip Sheet: Faith Communities & Disaster Mental Health" (New York: National Disaster Interfaiths Network, 2007).

[22]Roberts and Ashley, *Disaster Spiritual Care*; SAMHSA, "Tips for Disaster Responders: Understanding Compassion Fatigue" (Rockville, MD: SAMHSA, 2014), HHS Publication No. SMA-14-4869; SAMHSA, "Preventing and Managing Stress: Tips for Disaster Responders" HHS Publication No. SMA-14-4873. (Rockville, MD: SAMHSA, 2014).

[23]Adapted from M. E. Copeland, *Dealing with the Effects of Trauma: A Self-Help Guide*, SAMHSA-3717; SAMHSA, *A Guide to Managing Stress in Crisis Response Professions* (Rockville, MD: SAMHSA, 2005), SMHSA-05-4113; SAMHSA, *Field Manual for Mental Health and Human Service Workers in Major Disasters* (Rockville, MD: SAMHSA, 2005), ADM90-0537; S. Harding, *Spiritual Care and Mental Health for Disaster Response and Recovery* (New York: New York Disaster Interfaith Services, 2007).

9 Case Studies in Disaster Ministry

[1]Case study authors: David Boan, Hazel Rosete, Jessica Polson and Jamie D. Aten.

[2]Dan McCabe and Chris Schmidt, *Killer Typhoon*, Nova, aired January 22, 2014, www.pbs.org/wgbh /nova/earth/killer-typhoon.html.

[3]Case study authors: Joseph Kimmel, Youngok Kim, David Boan, Jamie D. Aten and William Clearly.

[4]Case study authors: Jamie D. Aten, David Boan, Kari Leavell, Scott Stegman, Joseph Kimmel and William Livingston.

10 Conclusion

[1]N. M. Roth, *Nehemiah Response: How to Make It Through Your Crisis* (Mustang, OK: Tate Publishing, 2009).

[2]B. Graham, *Storm Warning: Whether Global Recession, Terrorist Threats, or Devastating Natural Disasters, These Ominous Shadows Must Bring Us Back to the Gospel* (Nashville: Thomas Nelson, 2010).

[3]Southern Baptist Convention Disaster Relief, "Church Preparedness for Disaster Relief" (North American Mission Board).

Permissions Information

Anyone wishing to photocopy or reproduce material from *Disaster Ministry Handbook* by Jamie D. Aten and David M. Boan must obtain written permission from InterVarsity Press (with the exception of groups that meet all of the criteria outlined below). Permission may be requested by writing permissions@ivpress.com or:

Permissions
InterVarsity Press
P.O. Box 1400
Downers Grove, IL 60515

Exception

Some portions of this book are intended to be photocopied for noncommercial congregational disaster preparedness use. Nonprofit groups that meet all of the following criteria may make print photocopies of those worksheets clearly labeled for such use without written permission:

1. The group making and distributing photocopies of the worksheets is a church or other nonprofit group.

2. No fee is charged for any of the distributed materials.

3. The group making and distributing the photocopies owns a copy of *Disaster Ministry Handbook.*

4. The published credit line is included on all copies of the copied materials.

5. No change or alteration may be made.

If there are to be exceptions to any of the above terms, then written permission is required from InterVarsity Press. Exceptions include, but are not limited to, making and/or distributing digital copies, republishing in another publication, translating and selling copies.

About the Authors

Dr. Jamie D. Aten (PhD, Indiana State University) is the founder and codirector of Wheaton College's Humanitarian Disaster Institute and Dr. Arthur P. Rech and Mrs. Jean May Rech Associate Professor of Psychology at Wheaton College (Wheaton, Illinois). Previously he served as the assistant director of the Katrina Research Center and as an assistant professor of psychology at the University of Southern Mississippi. Dr. Aten first became involved in applied disaster research and training after moving to South Mississippi just six days before Hurricane Katrina struck. Within a few weeks he became active in studying and joining the church and community response to address the overwhelming spiritual and emotional needs left behind in the wake of the storm. Since that time, through various roles and capacities, he has been active in responses to a number of other disasters, including Hurricanes Rita and Gustav; H1N1 pandemic; 2010 Mississippi Delta and 2011 Alabama Tuscaloosa tornadoes; civil unrest in the Democratic Republic of the Congo, Liberia and Kenya; Deepwater Horizon oil spill; Japan and Haiti earthquakes; and Philippines typhoon. Dr. Aten has been awarded over $4 million in external funding by numerous state, federal and nonprofit organizations to study and support disaster preparedness and response activities of churches and faith-based organizations around the globe. For his work with faith-based organizations after Hurricane Katrina, he was recognized with the Mutual of America Merit Finalist Award. More recently, he received the American Psychological Association's Division 36 (Psychology of Religion) Margaret Gorman Early Career Award for his research on the psychology of religion/spirituality and disasters. He has published over one hundred articles or chapters and made over two hundred professional presentations. He is also the coeditor or coauthor of eight books and has served as a guest coeditor of several special professional journal volumes, including an issue on faith and trauma in the *Journal of Psychology and Theology*. Follow Dr. Aten on Twitter: @drjamieaten.

Dr. David Boan (PhD, Biola University) is codirector of the Humanitarian Disaster Institute at Wheaton College (Wheaton, Illinois) and associate professor of psychology in the Wheaton College Graduate School of Psychology. He is a clinical psychologist with over thirty years' experience in applied health care research, international psychology, organizational development and performance improvement. After receiving his PhD in 1978 in clinical psychology from the Rosemead Graduate School of Psychology at Biola University in California, Dr. Boan entered clinical practice in Sacramento, California. In addition to direct clinical services, his work included building church capacity for community programs, including programs for underserved and disabled people. After twenty years of clinical work, Dr. Boan became vice president of the Delmarva Foundation for Medical Care in Maryland, where his work focused on health care improvement. In 2006 he joined the Joint Commission Resources in Oak Brook, Illinois, as executive director for innovation. His work with JCR included designing services to enhance organizational capacity for quality and safety, sustaining performance improvement, and developing guidelines for quality care in developing countries. In 2011 Dr. Boan joined Dr. Jamie Aten as codirector of the Humanitarian Disaster Institute at Wheaton College. Dr. Boan leads a research program, supervises student research and teaches consulting psychology, history and systems, and research design and program evaluation. He currently manages grants for building church capacity for disaster care in Japan, the Philippines and Kenya, and works with the University of Notre Dame in Haiti to develop trauma treatment for children and build community capacity for mental health care. He is the author of more than fifty professional papers and presentations in psychology.

About the Humanitarian Disaster Institute

Humanitarian
DISASTER INSTITUTE

Wheaton College's Humanitarian Disaster Institute (HDI) is the country's first faith-based academic disaster research center. HDI is a college-wide interdisciplinary research center dedicated to helping equip domestic and international congregations and faith-based organizations to prepare for, respond to and recover from disasters and humanitarian crises. HDI carries out this mission through research, training and technical support.

Contact Information

We welcome inquiries from individuals and organizations interested in finding out more about our programs and services, as well as from those interested in collaborating with us.

The Humanitarian Disaster Institute
Psychology Department
Wheaton College
501 College Ave.
Wheaton, IL 60187
Phone: (630)752-5104
Email: hdi@wheaton.edu
Website: www.wheaton.edu/HDI

 facebook.com/HDIWheaton

 twitter.com/WheatonHDI

IVP PRAXIS

EQUIPPING LEADERS FOR MINISTRY

"...TO EQUIP HIS PEOPLE FOR WORKS OF SERVICE,
SO THAT THE BODY OF CHRIST MAY BE BUILT UP."

EPHESIANS 4:12

God has called us to ministry. But it's not enough to have a vision for ministry if you don't have the practical skills for it. Nor is it enough to do the work of ministry if what you do is headed in the wrong direction. We need both vision *and* expertise for effective ministry. We need *praxis*.

Praxis puts theory into practice. It brings cutting-edge ministry expertise from visionary practitioners. You'll find sound biblical and theological foundations for ministry in the real world, with concrete examples for effective action and pastoral ministry. Praxis books are more than the "how to"—they're also the "why to." And because *being* is every bit as important as *doing*, Praxis attends to the inner life of the leader as well as the outer work of ministry. Feed your soul, and feed your ministry.

If you are called to ministry, you know you can't do it on your own. Let Praxis provide the companions you need to equip God's people for life in the kingdom.

www.ivpress.com/praxis